Praise for *The Embezzler,*

"*The Butcher, the Embezzler, and the Fall Guy* is a compelling book of family history, an urgent look inside the machinations of wealth and power, and a wonderfully well-written journey into a fully realized past. Cherington, the daughter of a poet and the granddaughter of an astute businessman, wields the many elements of her inheritance with grace."

—**Beth Kephart**, National Book Award finalist and author of *Wife | Daughter | Self: A Memoir in Essays*

"In this fascinating historical memoir, Gretchen Cherington sets out on a determined quest to discover why her grandfather, who played a pivotal role in the early success of the Hormel meat company, was ultimately forced out of the company. To understand this pivotal event that forever changed her family's fortunes, Gretchen returns to her midwestern roots to uncover the truth about the meatpacking industry and the powerful men who shaped it. Engrossing me from first page to last, this is a compelling mystery of corporate greed, family legacy, and a granddaughter's search for answers."

—**Laura Davis**, author of *The Courage to Heal* and *The Burning Light of Two Stars*

"Cherington's second book is a fascinating blend of history, family biography, and personal memoir. Who knew the Hormel company's history was so infused with drama and intrigue? Cherington is a meticulous researcher with keen insights into human flaws and subtleties, born of her professional training in consulting work. She is also a woman on a soul-searching quest into her own family's shadowy past. A poetic sensibility infuses Cherington's prose, making this engaging, multidimensional story a highly compelling read."

—**Robin Clifford Wood**, author of *The Field House: A Writer's Life Lost and Found on an Island in Maine*

"Cherington dismantles myth after myth in this visceral and emotional story, one complicated by family legacies large and small that are twined by love and loss. At the book's center, a small town that orbits around buttoned-up businessmen and an industry that feeds the nation's bellies with slaughtered hogs."

—**Kerri Arsenault**, author of *New York Times* Editors' Choice *Mill Town: Reckoning with What Remains*

"Engagingly written, combining elements of history, memoir, and mystery. This book is a delight."

—**Monica Wood**, author of *The One-in-a-Million Boy*,

"With crisp writing and an eye for detail, Cherington masterfully weaves a story of ambition, intrigue, and family legacy. Equal parts mystery and memoir, Cherington's curiosity takes her to the farmlands and feedlots of southern Minnesota as she unearths shocking and long-hidden details of this true-crime tale. I was totally hooked."

—**Bob Keyes**, author of *The Isolation Artist: Scandal, Deception, and the Last Days of Robert Indiana*

"I'm not often a reader of history, but *The Butcher, the Embezzler, and the Fall Guy*, with its blend of fact and memoir and family lore, kept me entranced. Through her vivid prose and clear-eyed honesty, Cherington guides readers skillfully back to a time and place that bustles with life—a trip I would take again and again with this talented author."

—**Cheryl Suchors**, author of *48 Peaks: Hiking and Healing in the White Mountains*

"What happens when we unravel family myths? In her newest memoir, *The Butcher, the Embezzler, and the Fall Guy*, Gretchen Cherington finds no easy answers as she unfolds a true crime tale concerning a grandfather she never knew. As we're drawn into this intricate story of high life and deceit in the early twentieth century, both author and reader wonder if Cherington's grandfather was complicit in an embezzlement scheme that rocked a name-brand company. With characteristic honesty, and relevant to readers everywhere, Cherington's powerful prose prompts us to look at our own family stories in new ways."

—Ashley E. Sweeney, author of *Hardland*

THE BUTCHER,
THE EMBEZZLER,
AND THE FALL GUY

THE BUTCHER, THE EMBEZZLER, AND THE FALL GUY

A Family Memoir of Scandal and Greed in the Meat Industry

Gretchen Cherington

SHE WRITES PRESS

Published 2023
Printed in the United States of America
Print ISBN: 978-1-64742-083-3
E-ISBN: 978-1-64742-084-0
Library of Congress Control Number: 2022920596

For information, address:
She Writes Press
1569 Solano Ave #546
Berkeley, CA 94707

Interior Design by Tabitha Lahr

She Writes Press is a division of SparkPoint Studio, LLC.

Images on pages 27, 28, and 113 are owned by Hormel Foods Corporation, its subsidiaries, and affiliates, and used by permission. © Hormel Foods, LLC.

Images on pages 112 and 136 are used by permission of the Hormel Historic Home, Austin, Minnesota.

Image on page 77 is used by permission of the *Austin Herald*.

Images on pages 56 (right), 75, 97, 114, 116 (bottom), and 140 are used by permission of the Mower County Historical Society.

Image on page 244 © Shutterstock.com.

All other images are provided by the author.

World rights for *Orchard*, by Richard Eberhart, are provided by the Richard Eberhart Literary Estate. American rights are provided by Oxford University Press.

The 1921 article from *The Squeal* on page 211 is courtesy of the author's family archives. Originally published by Geo. A. Hormel & Company.

In loving memory of the grandparents I never knew,
Alpha LaRue and Lena Lowenstein Eberhart

And for my family,
past, present, and future

What is history but a fable agreed upon?
—NAPOLÉON

Everywhere, the land is not ours.
Everywhere, the past has a dark underbelly.
Everywhere, what appears to be
one thing is something else.
—ANGELA PALM

Contents

Author's Note

This is a work of memory, research, and my imagination. I am indebted to the Richard Eberhart Literary Estate for permission to use its source materials at Dartmouth College's Rauner Special Collections Library, which include my grandfather A.L. Eberhart's personal letters and business documents. Without those I would not have found his voice for this book. At Dartmouth, I was assisted by former staff member Sarah Hartwell and current librarian Jay Satterfield. My Eberhart cousins have shared family letters, journals, photograph albums, and stories about our grandparents whom none of us knew. Each was a source of vital information, history, and opinion.

Memory is fallible and subject to interpretation. Even in primary sources, some facts of this story conflict. Sometimes I have chosen to acknowledge this; sometimes I have chosen the fact I feel best matches what I have come to believe is true. Where quoting primary sources, I have used italics and, where needed, edited lightly for ease of reading. I have used a single letter to identify certain persons to protect their privacy.

The original research for this book took place during three trips to Austin, Minnesota, between 1995 and 2000, and five years thereafter. Between 2018 and 2022, I expanded the research with generous assistance from individuals in Austin and elsewhere. Any errors are mine alone.

Geo. A. Hormel & Company, now often thought of as Hormel Foods, prefers to be referred to by its original name. Where possible in the narrative flow, I have honored that preference. At other times I've referred to the company simply as Hormel, or the Hormel company, as it was not known as Hormel Foods at the time of this story.

This work is neither intended to be a definitive biography of any of the three protagonists, nor a complete history of the first twenty years of Geo. A. Hormel & Company. It is impossible to know the exact truth of events that occurred one hundred years ago, or their full impact through the generations that have followed.

1.

Flimsy Pretext

Austin, Minnesota

1922

In late January 1922, Alpha LaRue Eberhart peered out the multi-paned windows of George Hormel's executive office in Austin, Minnesota, at the Red Cedar River below. The river was frozen stiff as death, splitting the meatpacking town in two. The afternoon temperature had barely risen since daybreak. A biting wind drove across the plains, blowing clouds of snow and factory steam eastward and rattling the windows' glass.

I imagine A.L., as my grandfather was called, stood his ground, undaunted, eyes sure, as he was forced to resign from the company he had spent twenty years helping to build. The men's words were brief that day. A.L. knew there was no point in arguing with his high-strung boss. George Albert Hormel was unlikely to change his mind. Maybe that day, as in photographs, George's right hand palmed his thigh, his fingers spreading south, as if ordering a dog to sit.

George's skin was paler than A.L.'s, his hair thicker and parted left to right, his nose nearly piercing his upper lip. His pinched eyes nipped the skin behind his wire-rim glasses, conjuring a scolding teacher dressing down an errant student. When the ticking clock on his wall struck the next hour, packinghouse workers would hang up their aprons and head home. Despite the bespoke suits and starched shirt collars worn by these men, theirs was a killing business—an abattoir that turned plump animals into food, splattering blood on the meatcutters' aprons and dropping guts into buckets on the floor.

The facts leading up to my paternal grandfather's forced resignation were clear. Six months earlier, the company had discovered a nearly $1.2 million embezzlement by its star comptroller, Ransome Josiah Thomson. The defalcation, as it was called back then, had taken place over the course of nearly a decade. Newsprint across thirteen hundred cities had inked the story, with the *New York Times* headline reading: *Report Shows Embezzler Got $1,187,000.* After the embezzlement, the value of one share of Hormel stock plummeted almost to zero, scattering the company's assets and reputation to the wind, putting at risk a thousand employees and cratering my grandfather's personal wealth, much of it in Hormel stock. As A.L. watched Thomson being marshalled off to jail, town gossip swirled like eddies of pork fat draining off the Hormel cutting floor.

That January day, my grandfather trudged out to his Cadillac Suburban, hauling up the collar of his heavy, Chicago-tailored, wool topcoat against the cold. Snowdrifts felted his pant legs. Even the howling blow couldn't entirely conceal the sound of squealing pigs being prodded from outdoor pens onto the killing floor at the back of the factory.

Across the Red Cedar River, A.L. pulled up the long, winding driveway to his estate. Snowfall blanketed the regal white peonies he and his wife, Lena Lowenstein, had planted three years earlier, which lit up the month of June each summer like puffy clouds dancing over the southern

Minnesota plains. The couple's second son—seventeen-year-old Richard, who would become my father—ever hopeful for his father's afternoon return from work, was shoveling drifts from the family's front veranda. Inside their lavish home, Lena lay dying.

Whatever my grandfather said to his family about being fired that day—for it had been a "resignation" only in George Hormel's imagination—he penned a letter to his closest friend and business confidant, George Hastings Swift, heir to the giant Chicago meatpacking company Swift & Company: *You will probably be as much surprised as I was to know I have resigned my position, requested by Mr. Hormel on what seemed a very flimsy pretext.*

GEORGE HORMEL'S "FLIMSY PRETEXT," and my grandfather's firing, were legend in my family. My father cast them as Shakespearean tragedy—or the Horatio Alger story, if Alger had lost his American dream. Six decades after the events, my father still wept when describing his father's fall from grace and his mother's early death to cancer. Thomson's embezzlement in Austin, Minnesota, and the weight of company and family shame were traumas for my father which got taken up by me.

As a kid, I was spellbound by Dad's telling of the events, but by the mid-1990s, when I was in my forties, I was reckoning with the complicated man I knew him to be—a Pulitzer Prize–winning poet who surrounded himself with the best writers of the twentieth century, from Robert Frost to James Dickey; a man who championed women poets and loved my mother deeply yet had engaged in multiple affairs throughout his marriage and had on one occasion, when I was seventeen, molested me in my bedroom. He was my first experience of a powerful, confusing man. He was known for telling stories that entertained his fans, but I'd learned as an adult that some of those stories were exaggerated and others simply untrue. While his tales calcified into family myth, I no longer knew whether to trust them, or his tears.

By all accounts, my father and his two siblings enjoyed an idyllic childhood in Austin, but the idyll ended that bitter January day when A.L. was called to George Hormel's office.

If my father polished his stories with the élan of the literary star he would become, I was looking for a way to square them with my own lived experience. I wanted to understand my midwestern legacy within the broad sweep of its geographic scale and our early nation building.

I never knew my paternal grandparents. Both died long before I was born. I didn't really know what to believe about Alpha LaRue Eberhart, George Hormel, or Ransome Thomson. What I knew was that throughout my early career as a management consultant, as I partnered with CEOs—mostly men, back then—stories of the three men in Austin haunted me. I was working with clients to help them change their companies into places where both business and people could thrive. I watched how the CEOs operated, learned how they made decisions, took in how they told their own stories, each one of them giving me a reference point against which to think about my grandfather.

If my father poetically described his father as *six feet of manhood and not a mark of fear*, few top executives I knew had no fear. If my father cast George Hormel as the villain—*a bastard, all greed for laying [his] father so low*—I knew such descriptions were rarely that clean. As for the embezzler, my father both marveled at his ingenious stealing and railed at his audacity but chose to blame him less than he did his father's former boss.

In forty years advising hundreds of powerful men, I had occasionally been in their corner suites as they considered a firing. I knew their primary reasons. Now I wanted to know how Geo. A. Hormel & Company, a brand-name business that would become the $11 billion conglomerate it is today, got started; how the fates of these three men were sealed on the banks of the Red Cedar River; how a company nearly brought to its knees in 1921 was declared by its bankers as too big to fail; and what role any of this had to do in shaping me.

2.

Company Town

Austin, Minnesota

1995

Out the window of our compact rental car, soybean fields stretch like billowing sheets on a laundry line. My cousin Eloise Eberhart and I are traveling on Interstate 35 from the Minneapolis airport to Austin, one hundred miles south.

Blessed with a crop of thick salt-and-pepper hair and blushed cheeks, El is a classic beauty with the dark brows of our grandmother and the dancing eyes of our grandfather. At sixty, she is fifteen years my senior. That used to matter when she was twenty-five and I was ten, but it doesn't now. We've set aside three days to explore this place our fathers reminisce about, and I hope to leave with a clearer story of what happened here before either of us was born.

The cerulean sky is nearly free of clouds. Wisps of fluff sail untethered. Acres fly by so fast it's hard to catch their detail. The vast, open space of southern Minnesota is freeing, after the charming but sometimes claustrophobic hills of New Hampshire and a hefty consulting season. A kaleidoscope of questions hangs overhead as El drives and I stare out the window. Why, if Austin was so pivotal to our fathers, did neither of them ever bring us here? Dad's stories tangle in my brain like lines left unfurled on a sailboat. Maybe I'm just here to clear up a few of those lines.

"How old was I when I was your flower girl?" I ask El, having half-forgotten the details of a favorite memory. The photograph of me at her wedding is a cherished one—she in a fitted, virginal gown, me in my white dotted swiss beaming up at my beautiful cousin, squeezing her hand so tight I can feel the hurt.

"Ten," El says, her cheeks flushed the same pink as the bouquet of baby roses I clutched in two hands that day.

I fill El in on my consulting work. In tandem with my forty-fifth birthday, my company has just reached its ten-year mark. Friends tell me I work too much, but the long-term partnerships I've formed with CEOs as they transform their company cultures exhilarate me. I like seeing positive change happen.

Eloise is a fundraiser for the American Friends Service Committee, and lives in Chicago. She is sometimes called to southern Minnesota to meet with prominent donors and has been to Austin several times, where she has met people who knew—or knew of—our grandparents.

Staring out the window, I think of the summer I got as close to Austin as I ever have until now. In 1968, I was seventeen, away from home for two months, working on a service project with Mexican American migrant workers employed by the Owatonna Canning Company, a short jog northwest of Austin. A memory surfaces; I glance at El and share it with her.

Seasonal employees are packed hip-to-hip, I tell her, like standing pick-up sticks in the backs of open trucks, and driven to the fields where they will spend twelve hours harvesting asparagus and strawberries, bent over long rows in the hot sun.

I'm playing outside a single-room cinder-block home at the migrant camp with Maria and her toddler sister, Elena, while her older siblings and parents work in the fields. Maria is hungry and goes inside. A couple minutes later, I look through the open door and see her leaning over a gas flame, fixing a pan of something for Elena's lunch. Her cotton dress drapes too close to the flame and catches fire. The next thing I know, I'm rolling her in a blanket and the room stinks of singed cotton.

Just thinking of it, I'm shaken.

"It was terrifying," I say to El. "Looking back, I think it was the first time I realized my own privilege."

THE CLOSEST THING I KNOW TO THIS VAST Minnesota sky is the rose-washed reach of Penobscot Bay, Maine, where my family summered. Here, I feel like El and I are in a massive bubble, with a sky-colored circus tent overhead and soybeans stretching to earth's end. The bubble seems to contain today and every story we've heard about southern Minnesota from our fathers. But how strong is this bubble? And—knowing myself—how far will I go to find out?

El's mission for this weekend seems to be to set the family record right about our grandfather—that he was wronged by George Hormel. We've procured an appointment with the Hormel corporate archivist because we've heard that a rumor still floats around the company, and in some parts of Austin, that our grandfather was complicit in Ransome J. Thomson's embezzlement. Publicly, I can't believe that's true. Privately, I don't know what to believe, but I know my family's stories are rarely uncomplicated.

"It's not right what the company did," El says after we pass a sign indicating we're more than halfway to Austin. "Our grandfather was a *good* man. A family man. And *he built* that company."

"That's what we've heard," I say. "I never knew Dad to hate anyone, but he *hated* George Hormel. A.L. and George were friends. George's wife Lillian and Grandmother Lena were too. And Hormel fired A.L. while Lena was *dying*." I shake my head. "I don't know how our grandfather got through that year."

El sighs. "Me either."

The lush, weed-free miles of soybeans lull me. I hope I'm open to learning whatever I need to learn about my grandfather. I'm not here to prove his innocence. I've only started to look through the four large boxes of his letters and business documents held within my father's literary archives at Dartmouth College. I don't know what to believe, but I want to test a few nascent speculations while I'm here. Like it or not—and sometimes I don't—I've always wanted to know the truth about everything. A new entrepreneur client once told me that trait might get me in trouble in the short run but was the only way to live. The CEOs with whom I consult want the truth I see inside their companies. It's only when they're grounded in reality that they can make their best decisions.

If family lore holds that A.L. was devastatingly wronged by his boss, did my grandfather own any part of it? If George Hormel was a bastard, as my father said, might he have been anything more? Maybe my grandfather was neither the saint my father described nor the sinner George Hormel fired.

A falcon glides east across the highway, makes a hard north turn, and traces his beady eyes to the ground, scouting for dinner. What was my grandfather scouting for in 1901 when he accepted George Hormel's invitation to Austin? What could the young Hormel, a novice entrepreneur, have offered that was attractive enough to lure A.L. from a good job with an already giant meatpacking company in Chicago, a city known as the meat capital of the world?

By 1901, A.L. was heading up Swift & Company's sales offices in St. Paul. Newly married, and known in the industry, he had a bright future ahead of him. St. Paul was a bustling city of 160,000 people with concrete sidewalks, broad streets, and trolley cars. Austin was a town of 5,000 with a muddy Main Street littered with fifteen saloons and three billiard halls.

The highway spills out ahead of us, splitting sixty miles of soybeans like the Red Cedar River splits the east and west sides of Austin. Ever since George Hormel opened his first meat market in 1898, Austin has been a company town. Now, the Hormel company is ranked among the ten largest meatpackers in the country, and is no longer run by family members. Under corporate leadership, it has reconstructed its brand, in part by accenting the second syllable of the family name instead of the first. Those we'll meet in Austin will still claim the family's pronunciation of *Hor*mel. At first, this sounds odd to my ear, an indication that the newly accentuated Hor*mel* has taken root, at least beyond Minnesota.

This weekend, El and I will discover that the company's smoked meats infuse nearly every block we will walk in Austin. Its history will show on the faces of most citizens we encounter. Its brand plumps the bellies of white, midlevel executives who fill city restaurants from noon to one o'clock. Its name or its money is associated with the high school auditorium, the 4,000-seat high school football stadium, the nature center, the golf course, the library. Riverland Community College fills its classes with hopeful eighteen-year-olds ready to work for the company in entry-level positions. There wouldn't be much to Austin, Minnesota, without Geo. A. Hormel & Company, which makes the company both powerful and incapable of hiding.

AT SOME POINT, THE SOYBEANS OUTSIDE OUR car turn into oats, and millions of seed heads bob like the ends of upside-down brooms. If I squint just right, I can turn those oats into the fur underbelly of a hog. Squint and release. Squint and release. I lock in this image of place, where endless feed crops surround a town whose name is synonymous with bacon.

"It's beautiful here," I say. "This big sky. These endless waves of grain." The cliché feels right.

"*Oh beautiful for spacious skies,*" El sings in her perfect soprano, her patriotism contagious. There's a lot of amber grain here to admire.

"So different from the shrimpy farming valleys of New England," I say, laughing. "A family farm in New Hampshire would be a backyard 4-H project here. We can't hold a candle."

El and I tally a list of questions for the weekend. We line up the first two men in our sights: George Albert Hormel, with his stolid Germanic frame, his five-pound meat cleaver hanging from his butcher's belt; Alpha LaRue Eberhart, with his perfect posture and patrician nose, his sizzling eyes, his show tunes piano-playing that charmed Lena Lowenstein of White Hall, Illinois, into marrying and following him to downtown Chicago, to St. Paul, and finally to Austin.

"You know, we could have been rich," I say, leaning into El. "Really rich. I figured it out. From the financial records in Dad's archives. If A.L. had been able to hang on to his Hormel stock, we'd be filthy rich, just like George Hormel's grandchildren."

"But money . . ." El smiles, she the frugal wife of a minister. "It might have corrupted us!"

I could stand a little corruption right now, I think to myself. My divorce five years ago, my two children headed to college, my growing consulting company—money flowing in is just about matching money flowing out. I don't know what I feel about the level of wealth we might have inherited, but my curiosity here has never been about the lost money, even if the specter of it is seductive. Really, it is about these three protagonists who've occupied my family stage. I feel a need to inhabit them, to try to understand who they were, what they did, and why—to the extent that's even possible. I want to claim the grandfather and grandmother I never knew. I want to tell their story as I figure out mine.

El signals our exit from the highway. "You read the directions, Gretch." She hands me a printed email from Betty Catherwood, the woman whose house we're looking for.

A few commercial outfits sprinkle the edge of the highway exit, then there's just a flat grid of unremarkable neighborhoods, one after another, as we head into town. We could be anywhere in Iowa, Wisconsin, Nebraska. Middle America. In 1995, this small city of 20,000 doesn't offer much of a first impression.

3.

He Could Cleave a Hog with a Single Blow

Austin, Minnesota

1995 and 1900

Betty Catherwood uncorks a bottle of dry sherry and places a platter of mini hot dog buns stuffed with something mayonnaise-y between El and me. We're tired from traveling but eager to be with Betty, whose husband, Roger, died last year. Rog Catherwood was our fathers' best friend growing up in Austin.

"See what you think of these," Betty says, offering her platter.

I'm not sure what I'm looking at.

"I thought we'd start with Spam," she says.

"Spam!" El's laugh trills through the room like her song.

The mention of Spam is enough to wake me from jet lag. Hormel's best-known product, created after A.L. left the company, made famous for feeding soldiers during World War II, then infamous by Monty Python. My mother made Spam sandwiches on island picnics in Maine. She called it the perfect American food—a mash-up of whatever bits and pieces had no other home. "Like our nation," she'd laugh, "with its 'tired and poor.'"

The little sandwiches are dressed up with mayonnaise, chopped pickles, scallion, and celery, then dusted with paprika, and I admit they are tasty.

Betty is a tidy, small, robust woman of seventy-five years whose thinning hair is colored and permed. Her pressed blue seersucker clothes offset her comfortable-looking beige walking shoes. A graduate of Wayne State University and an art teacher throughout her life, she is, according to El, open-minded, so I assume she won't mind my questions, even though she's related to the Hormel family by marriage. Roger's father, Samuel Doak Catherwood, was George Hormel's best friend and long-term legal counsel, also a good friend of A.L. George's sole son, Jay Hormel, carried Catherwood as his middle name. The Catherwoods, Hormels, and Eberharts occupied privileged space in Austin.

Betty says she wants to know what we're learning while we're learning it.

"I found a journal of my father's from 1919," I say. "Two years before the embezzlement made national headlines. He and Rog hiked up the Cedar River to camp out."

"Oh, I'm eager to hear!" Betty's eyes are lit with memories of her husband.

I recount what I've read of Dad's journal—that he and Rog were working in the packing plant that summer and had just earned twelve dollars and change for two weeks' wages. I use air quotes when I retell from my father's journal, that they'd been *stuffing George Hormel's sausages*. This gets a laugh from El and Betty. Dad and Rog were excited for an adventure, for the freedom of finding a campsite near Ramsey that they'd made the summer before.

"Was Dryden on that trip?" El asks, referring to her father.

"Just Rog and Dad," I say. "Two boys free of their parents and their boss. But the river sounds like it was really shallow. Is that true?" I ask Betty.

"Oh, yes," she says, "it's never been much of a river. Sometimes you can walk across it. Except when it floods, and then it's quite dangerous."

"I think Rog was seventeen, Dad fifteen. They'd signed a pact to try to find an old haunted house in Ramsey. *In the dead of the night*," I say with air quotes again. I've been steeped in Dad's journals and letters recently, doing research for my first book.

"Ramsey is five miles north of Austin," Betty tells us. She reminds me that she knows my father because he and Rog corresponded through their adulthoods. In 1971, when Dad was sixty-seven, Austin High School invited him to speak to the graduating class on the occasion of his fiftieth reunion. My parents stayed with the Catherwoods on that trip.

"I'm just so glad you're here," Betty says as we three clink glasses.

FRIDAY MORNING, BETTY SCRAMBLES EGGS and fries Hormel bacon in the electric pan by her sink. She's planned a downtown walking tour for us this morning.

We first stop at the Austin Public Library—the predecessor of which, Betty reminds us, our grandmother Lena and Lillian Hormel helped get started by planning and raising money from Andrew Carnegie.

Strolling Main Street, I'm struck by the tidy blocks of stores and businesses lining both sides of the street: a pizza shop, a Chinese restaurant, a breakfast place, law offices, a gift store, a print shop, a hardware store. Everything you'd need, I guess, if you lived a hundred miles from Minneapolis and forty miles from Rochester. As we walk, Betty introduces us to Austinians we pass on the street. She knows nearly everyone and describes us to friends as "A.L. Eberhart's granddaughters," here to learn about the "Thomson years." Eyes widen and several men halt their morning strolls. Seventy-five years after Cy Thomson's embezzlement, his is still a big story here. Those who knew George Hormel personally—or knew of him through their parents who worked at the company—are eager to share their views of him.

"A dictator," one man says. "And rarely a benevolent one."

"He was a bully from what I heard," another says. "We all know your grandfather was wronged. He was the brains behind the company. You can be sure of that."

I'm resisting being sure of anything. I can't help but warm to these kind citizens coming to A.L.'s defense—still, how much of what they're saying about George Hormel is hearsay?

We arrive at a print shop and Betty pops in to invite its owner out to the street, away from the thrum of his press.

Knowles Dougherty is tall and lanky, with a straightforward smile. He seems interested in having a conversation. The slanting October sun lights up his face.

"George Hormel was known to be a mean man," Knowles asserts. "He was a German butcher by trade. He had powerful forearms. He could cleave a hog with a single blow."

I write that line in my notebook.

"Knowles's father is Richard Dougherty," Betty explains. "He wrote the two history books for the company's seventy-fifth and one-hundredth anniversaries."

"So, you have credibility," I say to Knowles. "And I'd love to read them."

"I'll get them to you, at Betty's," Knowles offers.

I ask Knowles about his background and learn that he and his wife founded the Warehouse Cooperative School, an alternative K–12 school in Boston where my cousin, Susan Butcher, the four-time winner of the Iditarod sled dog race in Alaska, went after dropping out of public school. He's a graduate of Swarthmore, with a PhD in education from Harvard. He's taught, farmed, published, and has now made his way back to Austin, where his parents are aging. His print shop keeps him busy. I like Knowles immediately. He's quirky and engaging. We have a quick back-and-forth about what I know about my grandfather.

"Just remember, Gretchen," he says before we part. "Mr. Hormel killed hogs for a living. He was big and tough. And," he repeats, "had powerful forearms."

I jot a crude sketch of big arms on my pad.

"He sounds intimidating," I say.

"He could be. He wasn't refined like your grandfather. He was a man with only one mission in life. What he cared about above all else was to succeed."

I file Knowles's name away as a possible ally in Austin and underline the word "succeed" in my notes. As we turn to leave, I say to El, "A man who cares above all else to succeed isn't a man who would admit failure."

BETTY LOOPS US BACK TO HER CAR and we head to The Old Mill Restaurant in an historic building at a sharp bend in the Cedar River. It's a dark room, somewhat brightened by windows on the river side. The hostess greets Betty with a happy lilt and welcoming hands. She steers us to a small, wooden table in the middle of the room with paper place mats and plastic-covered menus that don't appear to have been changed recently. A small vase of white carnations sits in the middle of the table.

Along one side of the restaurant is a long table set for lunch. Through the coming hour it will fill with men—no women—in their forties and fifties, each dressed in khaki slacks, dark loafers, and pastel-colored Oxford shirts. Middle managers, I presume, from the Hormel corporate offices. Their hair is trimmed, their midsections are soft, and their easy vernacular suggests they feel fortunate to work for this company and to live in this town. They remind me of midwestern men I've coached in executive education programs, ones noted by their human resources departments for their "high potential" to climb the corporate ladder. The best of them are sent to bolster their leadership skills at management finishing schools like Harvard, Columbia, and Dartmouth—campuses where consulting colleagues and I sometimes work as adjunct faculty. While the New Yorkers and Germans in our groups often bristle at what we teach, the midwesterners are rule followers, generally with positive attitudes. They're called "Midwestern Nice" for a reason. They may be wide-eyed in meeting their counterparts from Nigeria, Mumbai, Frankfurt, Tokyo, and London, but I like having them in my groups, as they usually don't make my job tougher than it needs to be.

Perusing the menu, I smile at El. "Doesn't look like we'll find much of a salad."

Down the menu runs a long list of Hormel meats: pork chop, pork butt, ham steak, ham sandwich, pork liver and bacon, pork stew, ham salad on iceberg lettuce, pork roast, and Spam burgers. I feel like a coastal food snob. But when I'm in foreign countries—and Austin does feel foreign—I eat what's put in front of me, and anyway we're here for the Hormel story, which is a story of meat, especially pork, so I settle for a ham sandwich on white bread with a pickle and chips.

The meat is soft and juicy—melt-in-my-mouth good.

AFTER LUNCH WE TAKE A BREAK BACK AT Betty's, where Knowles has already dropped off the two Hormel history books.

"They're here?" I say to Betty. I'm touched by Knowles's thoughtfulness and speedy delivery. I imagine his long legs jogging up to her door.

El and I move upstairs, where she nods off quickly. I pick up the books for my first fill of George Hormel.

George Albert Hormel was born in Buffalo, New York, on December 4, 1860, the year Abraham Lincoln was elected president. His parents, John Hormel and Susanna Decker, were members of a burgeoning community of industrious and pious German Americans in a city of nearly 80,000 people. Susanna came from a meatpacking family. John was employed in a tannery, where he would eventually become superintendent. Entrepreneurial by nature, John Hormel longed to own his own tannery, so in 1865, he and Susanna packed up their belongings, loaded all they owned in wagons, and placed the wagons on a lake boat bound for Toledo. George was their third-born of what would be a family of twelve children.

That year, just as the Civil War was ending, the family settled in a second-floor walk-up in Toledo. The small wooden building fronted an unpaved street and came with a messy backyard. Family furniture arrived late, and most of it was broken from the jostling it had sustained in the cargo hold during its journey the length of Lake Erie. There was no stove for heat until it could be fixed and the Hormel children slept on straw-stuffed pads on wooden slats on the floor.

The rough and teeming city of Toledo, population nearly 14,000, was built on the edge of a great swamp—part of the territory originally inhabited by the Ottawa and Seneca. Riddled with poverty, poorly constructed roads, and festering sewage, Toledo had no sanitary codes or building restrictions. There were no fire or police departments. There were no publicly funded schools. Families who could afford them housed livestock in their unmaintained yards. Tubs and sinks were unknown, as there was no running water. The Hormel privy was close to the well from which they pumped their drinking water.

At age seven, George was given the daily job of polishing the family's many pairs of shoes. One day, to save time, he polished only the fronts, figuring that was all that would show. His mother admonished him that no job should be "fudged"; if it wasn't done correctly on the first attempt, it would need to be redone. Later, George would write, *I learned it was quicker and easier to do the chore properly the first time.* He would carry that lesson with him when he started to build his company.

George was ten when he had to leave school to work in his father's tannery to help supplement the family income. First, he learned how to pull wool from sheep and to judge a sheepskin's grade. Then he learned to skin hides off pigs.

The Financial Panic of 1873 led to the closure of John Hormel's tannery, at which point thirteen-year-old George left home for good. Vagabonding through Kansas, Ohio, and Illinois, he picked up trade jobs in Cincinnati, Kansas City, and Chicago. He stretched and nailed wet sheepskins onto boards, laying thirty skins a day, for which he was paid two cents per square yard. He trimmed bones, made sausage, and dressed poultry for a meat market. None of these jobs lasted long. Exhaustion, hunger, and/or no bed to sleep on dogged him and precipitated his exit for something a little better, a little easier, or with a little more pay.

He worked as a dockwalloper on Lake Erie, unloading lumber and salt from cargoes. He became an assistant in the car shop of the Wabash Railroad. Frequently out of work for periods of time, he made do however he could. *I was no sunny optimist by nature*, he'd later claim. He had a low opinion of himself and never felt he did anything well enough. Occasionally, he returned to Toledo for his mother's warmth and a decent meal.

GEORGE HORMEL'S FIRST REAL JOB WAS provided by his maternal uncle, Jacob Decker, in 1875. Decker, who cut quite a figure in his shaggy buffalo coat and bearskin cap, owned a small meat-packing plant in Chicago. At fifteen, George was shipped to him by train with a box of his mother's sandwiches and cookies. Chicago, then called the "gem of the prairie," looked otherwise to the young man, who was stunned by his first impressions. Staring out the train windows at the city's outskirts, he saw only abject poverty, extending for miles. Cheerless buildings, heaps of ash and refuse, and slag and grime lined the railroad tracks and the shores of Lake Michigan. Decker's house and business were on Chicago's famed South Side, where George was met with treeless streets and curtainless windows.

Over the next year, George would become a bit player in the dark world of Chicago stockyards, seeing it all from the seat of his uncle's two-wheeled delivery cart. His weekdays were spent in this gloomy environment, but on his off days he took the train to Chicago's North Side, where he strolled by the grand brownstones on Aldine Square and the newest Marshall Field's Store, located just down the street (most notable, he'd write, for its new and plentiful electric lights). It was in this part of Chicago that George could imagine what it might be like to live in such homes and to work for such a company. Someday, he thought, maybe he would.

Uncle Decker taught George that cleanliness in a packing plant was more lucrative than filth. "Clean food," Decker said, "doesn't spoil in a hurry." Dirty food did. His uncle thought the great packinghouses of Chicago—particularly the trio of giants Swift & Company, Armour, and Cudahy—were wasteful and inhumane toward both animals and workers. Their ready-for-market meats, he said, were often covered in flies. Decker's insights and lessons would have a profound impact on George's thinking about the future labor he hoped to employ and what it would mean to become a meatpacker himself.

In 1879, George took a temporary job in Kansas City as a wool and hide buyer for Major J.N. Dubois. In 1880, at the age of twenty, he landed a permanent job, also as a hide buyer, for Oberne, Hosick, and Company, Chicago's world leader in hides, tallow, wool, and fur. George's headquarters were in Des Moines, Iowa, but his buying territory included most of the state, plus southern Minnesota. This region of the country, with its prosperous and tidy farms, cast a quick spell on him. Here there was enough space for a poor city boy to think big. The open spaces soothed his nervous mind. *Minnesota's cool blue skies and meadows flecked with brilliant flowers were like water to a thirsty man*, he wrote.

Young George became known for working hard by day and playing hard at night. He made friends easily along his buying route and liked best the ones he met in Austin, Minnesota. Betty Catherwood's future father-in-law, Samuel Doak Catherwood—Doak, as he was called—was born in a pioneer cabin west of Austin in 1859. Of German and Norwegian descent, he became an attorney, and when George Hormel met him, he had a law office over the Austin National Bank. The Catherwoods and hundreds of other European immigrants brought their strong work ethic and interest in education, the arts, and literature to southern Minnesota.

Immigrants shaped their new home in the likeness of the countries they'd come from, and Austin, well-placed along the Cedar River and with a good rail line connecting it to Minneapolis and Chicago, grew into a culturally progressive small city.

Reflecting in his unpublished autobiography *The Open Road*, George would confess to having an *itch for gambling* during his early years in Minnesota, and while he enjoyed the verdant, rolling hills, he was also called by the fifteen saloons lining Austin's Main Street. The town boasted three newspapers and residents were talking up a new shoe factory, a paper mill, and a brick plant. George thought it would make a good permanent home.

Aside from working hard, George devoted energy to accretive activities in his new community. Despite the low opinion he would later claim to have had of himself, he was a leader from the start, forming a bachelor's club, a tennis club, and a tobogganing club. He organized summer dances and winter sledding parties for fellow young people. He coordinated bicycle tours of the countryside and arranged fishing events. All the while, he enjoyed gambling—especially betting and bluffing. It was only after several years that he realized he hadn't saved a cent from his wages and made the decision to give it up.

In 1887, George's best customer on his buying route, Anton Friedrich, experienced a fire in his Austin butcher shop and small packing plant. Friedrich was disinclined to reopen. George saw an opportunity to partner with Anton's son, Albrecht, to take it on—but he needed money to do so. He sought a loan from George Crandale, his boss at Oberne, Hosick, and Company.

"I'd like to borrow five hundred dollars from you," George said.

"What for?" Crandale replied. "You're already overdrawn here for $104."

"I know," George said, pulling bills from his pocket. "Here's $4. That leaves $100. Lend me $400 more. If I haven't paid you in six months, I'll come back and work it off."

Crandale shook his head.

"You're a good traveling man, George, but a businessman? That's something else, and cards and business, they don't mix."

"I'm through with cards. This is my chance to make more of myself, and you can help."

"You know," Crandale said, taking in his young employee, "I believe you mean it. I won't stand in your way."

Anticipating his move to Minnesota, George wrote to his mother from Stuart, Iowa, *I am sure of success at Austin. Don't think I am going to be a common everyday butcher—that isn't what I am going into—it is the pork packing business I am about to enter. So don't say I am a butcher but a pork packer. We must hold our head up in this world.*

With Crandale's backing, George left his employment to form the firm of Friedrich & Hormel. The *Austin Register* called the two men "hustlers" who had reopened a more commodious retail market on Bridge Street and their new packinghouse northeast of the Cedar River. It was believed they would provide a good market for local livestock and *cheap meat* for Austin residents. Like many partnerships, however, the men conflicted from the start. George's vision was grander than Albrecht's—George had set his eyes on building an authentic packinghouse that could one day rival the Houses of Swift, Cudahy, and Armour, as the big packinghouses were called.

In 1891, Albrecht and George parted ways. Albrecht retained the retail outlet, while George took over the small packinghouse, the start of something he hoped to make big.

THE SOIL AROUND AUSTIN WAS DEEP AND BLACK, prime agricultural land in the heart of the American Midwest. Vast acreage was available for cheap, and easterners with gumption arrived in droves to settle there. Along with agricultural entrepreneurs came enterprising blacksmiths, grocers, doctors, and merchants. It was a big land for men with big ideas, and like most entrepreneurs, George Hormel was not deterred by what others might perceive to be the disadvantage of starting a small meat market in a city of 4,000, surrounded for miles by crop-growing land and 400 long miles from Chicago. George wagered he'd be close to small farmers raising quality animals, and with a better-than-average railroad system already laid across Minnesota, he imagined train cars filled with meats heading north and east.

George's tidy provisioner's market had an L-shaped counter that occupied two walls of its main room. The counter brimmed with fresh-cut Hormel meats and his signature smoked bacon. Sausage links hung from every rafter. Farmers outside Austin eagerly supplied their hogs and George cleaved every pig, cut up each carcass, and placed his meats on trays of ice on the counter. He tried to remember what his uncle Decker had taught him about handling, trimming, and curing meats. He'd seen too many crude and wasteful practices in butcher shops on his buying route. He reasoned, *If they can run a market profitably that way, how much better I'll do if things are run right.*

Business bustled from the start. Historians have attributed this early success to Hormel's frugality, thrift,

insistence on uniform product, and rigorous marketing and merchandising.

As one year turned to the next, George began hiring help for his counter and for killing and butchering his hogs. His meatcutters worked shorter than industry-average hours and were paid higher than industry-average wages. Maybe he needed these incentives to attract talent to a small town in southern Minnesota, but he was mostly seen as a decent employer who treated his workers better than they'd ever be treated in the Chicago stockyards.

George knew his way around the inside of a hog as well as any butcher in America. He trained his pointy eyes on innovating new cuts. In 1895, he found and created something no one had conceived of before.

Behind the shoulder of a hog is the loin, a highly desirable roasting cut, and the eye of the loin is the juiciest and sweetest morsel, with a smooth grain and good mouthfeel. George pondered that eye. His bacon was already selling well, and he wondered what might happen if he cured and smoked some of this leaner loin meat. He called it "Hormel's Sugar-Cured Pig Back Bacon" then; he's now credited with inventing what is known as Canadian-style bacon. By smoking and curing the eye of the loin, he added value to the cut—value his customers were happy to pay for. It was bacon without the fat. It was like eating a fine roast for breakfast. John Hormel's mantra to innovate, not imitate, would be a guiding force in George's packinghouse.

WHEN GEORGE HORMEL OPENED HIS SHOP in Austin, it was to the leading meat houses in Chicago what a pop-up coffee shop today might be to Starbucks: it might have better quality and taste, but it could never go head-to-head with a global brand. To get big, George knew he'd have to go toe-to-toe with the tough competition of Swift & Company and its founder, Gustavus Franklin Swift.

I knew about Gustavus Swift from my father. Swift, too, had opened a small meat shop, his in West Sandwich on Cape Cod, Massachusetts. He bought broken carcasses from the meat markets in Boston—carcasses of animals that had been shipped live by rail from Chicago, traveling nearly a thousand miles across half a dozen states in packed cars without cooling in summer or heat in winter, arriving in Boston underweight and bruised from bumping around with other pigs, if they were even alive. Swift saw this travel not only as rough on a live animal but also pricey, since he had to pay the whole animal's weight at the Boston stockyard even if he couldn't use some of its parts.

A frugal New Englander with a sharp eye for efficiency, Gustavus Swift saw that the place to be in meat production was where the animals were, in the Midwest, and especially

Chicago—so, in 1875, he uprooted his family and his business and moved west.

Swift would revolutionize the meat industry, first by turning on its head the idea of shipping whole, live hogs. While there'd been some experimentation with refrigerating a train car, Swift commissioned an all-new design specifically for carrying already butchered meat to eastern markets. Blocks of ice were dropped through roof hatches to chill the products on the floor below. Eventually, Swift would own seven thousand refrigerated railroad cars. Such ownership by a meatpacker didn't endear him to previous owners of that right—the railroads—but in his mind, it was his best way to gain control of shipping.

Swift was a tough industrialist who went on to play a pivotal role in the use of animal by-products for soap, glue, and fertilizer. He created early assembly lines that enabled mass production of meats, ever increasing his mechanized production, which would be picked up in other industries. He was known for instituting internal training programs to develop managers from within, and as an originator of the country's evolution toward national markets for major industrial products.

As an upstart entrepreneur, George Hormel was at the vanguard of independent meat packers that began moving the industry away from terminal "packingtowns" like Chicago, in favor of a direct buying route strategy, where packers took advantage of their close proximation to purebred livestock. By 1900, with Doak Catherwood's legal help, George won the right to own refrigerated rail cars himself, under the province of the Interstate Commerce Commission (ICC), just as the big Chicago meatpackers had. With ice rail cars he could sell meats directly to housewives and provisioners at a stop, helping to build brand awareness.

The ICC's allowance for ice car ownership by larger meatpackers led to the closure of hundreds of local meat companies in the Midwest that were unable to compete. This was probably also a boon to young George Hormel.

Meanwhile, several years into his work at his small plant, George introduced his first mechanical elevator to simplify the job of moving carcasses. No longer would he need what he called "armstrong elevators," the half-dozen muscled men who lugged big carcasses up flights of stairs.

As the business grew, George quickly realized that he couldn't keep doing all the cutting work. In 1900, at the age of forty, he hung up his cleaver and devoted his efforts to management. He hired a packinghouse superintendent and four salesmen, three of whom were his brothers. To succeed, though, he needed sales leadership, the kind that not many in the industry had—someone with vision and merchandising expertise, with the stamina for aggressive growth. He wanted someone familiar with the industry who would inspire a salesforce.

Alpha LaRue Eberhart was known for these things at the House of Swift. With national industry connections, an innate ability to motivate young men in sales, and inside knowledge about shipping meat by refrigerated rail cars, A.L. was a singular talent, one who would have attracted the eye of any of Swift's serious competitors. George Hormel pinned his hopes for the future on my grandfather.

4.

Oakwood Cemetery

Austin

1995

El is waking from her nap, so I fill her in—line for line, breathlessly—on everything I've learned about George Hormel. "I had no idea he grew up so poor," I tell her.

It's late in the afternoon and Betty wants us to take a walk with her at Oakwood Cemetery, where our grandparents and great-grandparents are buried, as are George and Lillian Hormel, Samuel Doak Catherwood and his wife, and their son and Betty's husband, Roger Catherwood.

The expansive cemetery borders the Red Cedar River and is graced by overarching burr oak trees, a particular genus known in Minnesota for their dark green, waxy leaves in summer. Now, in October, the leaves are mostly brown. I've never spent much time in graveyards, but they're known for being good places to walk and reflect. With a map from the gate house, I look for my grandparents' stones while Betty and El head off to place flowers at Roger's marker.

Four modest rectangular blocks of granite sit flat against the ground at the Eberhart plot. There's A.L.'s parents, Joseph

Snyder Eberhart and Emma May Swift Eberhart. There's Alpha LaRue and Lena Eberhart. I crouch to touch the simple rocks, to feel the cool, rough granite abrade my fingers. It's the closest I've ever been to these forebears. I wonder again why my father never brought me here. Seeing, carved in stone, how young my grandmother Lena was when she died, just forty-eight, brings tears to my eyes. I lay flowers between the markers. Not far away from where I stand is the twenty-five-foot-tall monolith that memorializes George and Lillian Hormel.

The river pulls me to where it separates the two sides of town, and I find a grassy spot to sit on its west bank. I'm glad for this lulling water, the pungent scent of burr oak leaves above me, my mind full of emerging perceptions of George Hormel. But if my head is with him, my heart is now with my grandfather and grandmother. Thinking of A.L.'s forced resignation from the Hormel company gets me thinking about being fired once myself.

In my case, I was called to the office of a consulting client. "We have things to talk about," my client said over the phone.

When I arrived at the small conference room, my first alarm was in seeing not just my primary client but four stone-faced executives sitting around the table.

"Gretchen, come sit."

Through the next thirty minutes, we didn't "talk" so much as one of the executives berated me as she became increasingly red-faced. This wasn't a firing in a few words, like my grandfather's. I could hardly find a space to speak, though, like A.L., I knew there was no point in arguing. They were unlikely to back down. Halfway through this executive's oration, I realized that what she was saying reflected things I'd heard from the company's employees over the prior several months.

I'd been brought in to canvass their workers. The company wanted to know if its employees were well enough prepared for its anticipated next stage of growth. The company had a strong brand, a loyal customer following, and high-quality products, but employee morale had plummeted after a spate of firings that the company owners had deemed essential. The remaining employees were watching their backs, worried about the security of their jobs, which led them to keep to themselves about quality issues and inefficiencies. There was fear of being let go, with no knowledge of what they were doing wrong.

I'd seen this before in family-owned businesses, where the company would assume, as it grew past its first hundred employees and toward multiple physical sites, that the same parochial communication practices used with twenty employees would work with hundreds.

As the owner's emissary carried on, I understood that just as the employees had crossed an unidentified boundary, I had too: I'd been too candid about what I'd heard inside. The company had *said* it wanted my true assessment, but I'd failed to notice a hesitation in the owner's voice when he said it.

Being fired hurt. I felt humiliated and concerned for my reputation as a start-up consultant. Back at my office, I called my mentor, Dan, then executive vice president of a global human resources company whose regional office was in Manchester, New Hampshire. We made an appointment to meet later in the week.

Dan was a large man, both in height and girth. I'd met him in business school, where he'd served as an outside advisor to MBA students. He had a huge heart and decades of human talent experience across three continents. At the top of the tallest building in the state, the glass walls of his office looked over the Amoskeag River and its iconic five-story brick mill buildings, symbols of a dying woolen industry.

"So," he said. "Tell me what happened."

I told the whole story, from the beginning.

"I'll say one thing," he said when I was done. "If you're not fired by at least one client a year, you're probably not pushing hard enough."

"Really?" I leaned forward. "Say more."

"Clients pay you well for your advice, but they won't always like hearing it." He shrugged. "If you're good, you're pushing people to be better, to do things differently—and some will resist. Look at it this way, if you didn't tell them what you heard, you'd be colluding in their dysfunctional system. It would have been a waste of their money and your time. The company's clearly not ready for the hard work of changing its culture—at least, not now."

I STAND UP FROM THE GRASS BY THE RIVER and stretch my legs, ready to find El and Betty. I'm beginning to unpack the family story in this meat town, and to see parallels with my own, but so much mystery remains.

"Hi, hon," El says. "How was the river?"

"Made me think about the time I got fired by a client," I say. "Which got me thinking about A.L. Remember how he'd invested in land around Austin? And his prize-winning herd of Holsteins? He was doing that outside of his job at the Hormel company. Maybe Mr. Hormel never clearly told him he couldn't. Maybe A.L. got fired because he'd crossed a line Hormel should have clearly laid down to him. Or what if, after twenty years, their partnership, like his with Albrecht Friedrich, had just gone stale? Makes me wonder if, even without an embezzlement, he might have been fired anyway?"

5.

Spam Town, USA

Austin

1995

On our last day in Austin, El and I make our way downtown to the Spam Museum. It's Monday morning and we're here to meet with Geo. A. Hormel & Company archivist V., whose office is at the back of the building. El told V. that we wanted to see all newspaper articles from around the time of our grandfather's firing. On the phone, V. implied that Cy Thomson and A.L. were in cahoots over the embezzlement—that A.L. had known Cy was stealing. El clarified that our family does not believe that was the case.

Occupying a prime location in Austin, the Spam Museum is a modern, peacock-blue box building in the shape of a can of Spam with the product's name emblazoned in large yellow letters on the front wall. Approaching the entrance, we take in a near life-size bronze statue of a hog farmer of yesteryear, dressed in overalls, with a pail in one hand and a prod in the other. He's following two bronze hogs walking side by side who don't look like they need any prodding. I've only raised pigs once, back in my hippie days, but they never walked in a straight line.

"Look, El," I say, poking at this company myth. "Genteel hogs heading off to slaughter with smiles on their faces."

Inside the museum are a dozen exhibits focused on Spam. "I ♥ Spam" is emblazoned on one wall as a backdrop for family photo ops. The "Spam Shack" sports surfboards on its wall, paying tribute to the Hawaiians who love Spam. The "Flying Pig" exhibits the flag from each of forty-four countries where Spam is consumed. Seventeen giant cans of differently flavored Spam, six to a row, are glued to a big open wall with a large **?** in the eighteenth spot, presumably to reinforce Hormel's reputation for continual innovation as the company carves out one more palate-satisfying flavor to satisfy a newly targeted demographic niche.

And, there's a corner devoted to Ransome J. Thomson and his embezzlement.

Even at 8:50 on a Monday morning, before the crowd arrives, it's a hoot of a museum, a whimsical cartoon creation of kitsch America designed to cement forever the company's wildly successful product in the minds of the 115,000 tourists who enter its doors every year, free of charge. Here you can even learn what a small blue can full of pork, sugar, water, salt, potato starch, and sodium nitrate can do for the soul.

El and I skip that exhibit.

Later, I'll learn that "Spam" came from a contest the company held after its invention in 1937. The winner was Kenneth Daigneau, brother of my father's boyhood friend Ralph Daigneau. Kenneth concluded the word "Spam" would convey what the product was—tasty **sp**iced h**am**. The company agreed, and Daigneau won $100.

Spam burst from the factory with spectacular sales. Today, it brings in $250 million in annual revenue for Hormel. About 3.8 cans of Spam are consumed every second in the

United States, which adds up to 120 million cans per year. A can of Spam is housed in the Smithsonian Museum and can be found on the shelves of one-third of all American homes. According to Bloomberg, via Marketplace, about 20,000 pigs are slaughtered every day to make all that Spam.

But we're not here for the Spam.

We meander through the displays to find V. in her office. In contrast to the museum, the archival suite has a corporate feel, with comfortable chairs and end tables stacked with Hormel PR puff pieces. Straight ahead of us is a half wall, behind which V. answers questions about Hormel history. Slim, trim, with frosted hair and about my age, she's wearing well-appointed, 1995-style business casual: a branded Hormel button-down shirt tucked into tan chinos. I note a large diamond engagement ring and wedding band on her left hand. She's a fitter version of the Hormel men we saw at The Old Mill Restaurant.

I let El take the lead. She thanks V. for her time, then asks, "So, what have you found? We're interested in anything related to our grandfather, Alpha LaRue Eberhart. We hope to understand why he was fired."

V. appears to bristle at the word "fired," but says, "Yes, I have what you asked for, here."

She fans a large stack of newspapers across a conference table like a deck of cards. I catch the scent of soft gray newsprint rising from the table. I love the smell of old paper.

Eloise and I paw through the pile, each picking articles to read, following from headlines to inside or back pages. We're looking for clues that would establish—in writing—a clear financial link between our grandfather and Cy Thomson, something documented that could justify A.L. being forced to resign.

About thirty minutes in, we start trading papers back and forth across the table while V. busies herself at her desk.

"I didn't find anything here," El says, "but you look."

"Neither did I. But I only skimmed that one, so you read it too."

El and I are distracted repeatedly by curiosities in these old newspapers—the sale of hogs, a social event hosted by the Ladies Club of Austin (of which our grandmother was a member), an addition planned for a church, Lena Eberhart entertaining friends at a luncheon in her home—an endless stream of small-town chatter. Now and then I lift my eyes and roll my neck. Outside the window, it's a beautiful, cloudless day.

After forty-five minutes, we've read about the company's prosperity through most of its first twenty years, as well as about the embezzlement, the Hormel company's dire straits because of it, and the shock of this scandal as it rippled across the nation. We're surprised by reports of an outpouring of public affection for Cy Thomson, despite his misdeeds, but scant mention of our grandfather, except for his resignation. None of this adds up to new information.

V. approaches us at the table, fidgeting with her rings.

"We're not finding anything here that ties our grandfather to the embezzlement by Thomson," El says.

Our first-ever look at actual newspaper reporting suggests Cy took full blame for the stealing, but V. reminds me of women I've worked with in dozens of companies who have something to say. In this era, they aren't often asked for their opinions. I ask her what she knows.

"My family goes back three generations with this company," V. says. "I've worked here since I was thirteen—except while away at college. So twenty-five years now."

I take in her sincerity and wonder what it would have been like if my father hadn't pursued a literary career and had remained in Austin. What if I'd been born here? Would I be more like V.? Might I be working for Hormel? She's worked her way up to this position of corporate trust, and pride softens her face as she speaks of her family. I interpret her words to mean that her family's made a good life here because of this company, and she's loyal to it.

"My family just said there *was* some kind of connection," she continues. "That's what I heard. Nothing very specific. Just that your grandfather was probably in cahoots with the embezzler."

"What do you mean 'cahoots'?" I ask.

"That maybe your grandfather was being protected by Thomson or that he was taking a kickback. That's why he was asked to resign."

"But we would have heard that if it were true," El protests.

I look at my cousin, wanting her claim to be right. But then, I've questioned other family stories. Maybe we've all just been enculturated to believe our grandfather was wronged.

V. pinches her lips. "I'm sorry I can't be more helpful to you."

"Well," El says, smiling, seeing she's not going to change V.'s mind, "I guess we'll have to leave it at that."

We thank V. again and I add, "I'll reach out if we have more questions," though I don't imagine I will. I've seen what the company has to offer, and I doubt I'll gain much more from pursuing this route.

IN THE RENTAL CAR HEADED NORTH TO the airport in Minneapolis, I say to El, "Well, she wasn't much help."

I stare out the window at the straight highway ahead of us. I love my cousin's conviction. It's what's made her such a good fundraiser and the social justice activist I admire. I know if we learn any bad news about our grandfather, we'll deal with it together. I wish I could leave it where she is. Maybe I'm just more practiced in reading between the lines of public corporate-speak and what is said inside companies privately, off the record. I've learned to interpret not just the words but the body language—and V.'s body language seemed sincere. If I want to know why our grandfather was fired, I need to look at everything. I venture a question to El.

"What if there *was* a connection? Just suppose. It's a small town. The company's growing fast, doing well. Three powerful men working side by side. We know Lillian Hormel and Lena were friends. We can assume George Hormel and A.L. were. Wouldn't it make sense they'd have both professional *and* personal relationships with Thomson and maybe know something that's not in the official record? But if A.L. knew about the embezzlement, then George Hormel must have known too."

"Huh . . ." El ponders my question. "Dad used to say how *decent* our grandfather was. That's all I heard, that his father had been wronged."

I'd like to cling to this family mythology too.

"But we both know that 'decent' and 'flawed' are not mutually exclusive," I say. "Look at my dad."

"True," El says.

Outside our windshield, everything is the same as three days ago—rows and rows of oats, now turning to soybeans as we head north, all bending toward the horizon, the overarching blue sky bright with sun, a bare whisper of cloud. But something feels new in me. Austin's residents have welcomed me. They've answered every question I've posed and generated more to think about. I feel stymied like water swirling around a plugged drain, but I want my effort to lead somewhere, and I think it could. I like these people. I like their town. I like this land. I'm intrigued by the Hormel history.

I have to assume this story of scandal and greed in the early 1900s comes with varying emotions. Yes, companies polish their reputations and skirt the line between candor and curated words to downplay their past. But if my family has posed one version of the Austin story, V. has hinted at another. For me, it's not about a possible connection between A.L. and Cy, since we know they had that through their work, but rather about whether my grandfather knew anything about the stealing, and about my family's insistence on mythologizing its men. Austin is no longer a distant metaphor for me, poetically resonant to my father. It's become real. I want to come back, to see it on my own terms.

El and I embrace before parting ways at the airport to catch our flights back to Chicago and New Hampshire.

"I never would have gotten here without you," I say in full embrace. "Forever thanks, Cuz."

"SIT BACK, RELAX, AND ENJOY THE FLIGHT," the pilot says. "It'll be a beautiful afternoon."

I fasten my seat belt and settle in, needing time to think. I'm exhausted from the accumulated miles of my last two weeks. Clients in Boston and New York, then in Hong Kong for three days with managers of the world's largest bank, then back briefly to New Hampshire, and out to Minneapolis and Austin. Now east again. I'm not sure which time zone I'm in or where I put my car when I left fourteen days ago. But it's not the physical exhaustion that's getting me. It's the emotional. I'm beginning to surface the fur underbelly of this family story and to let it breathe. Despite little detail, V. opened me up to something and I noted her confidence. Like everyone I met in Austin, she seemed honest.

Business executives have strong egos and vulnerabilities. Some are willing to look at these in order to keep them in check while making tough decisions. Some are disinterested in even acknowledging a shadow side. I'm no longer willing to accept the family lore without question; no longer willing to set aside my own intuition and experience. Culturally, especially as women, we put powerful men on pedestals, thinking they're better than us—but they're not.

But enough.

I lean back, close my eyes, and fall into a deep, much-needed, and good-for-the-whole-flight sleep.

6.

Six Feet of Manhood and Not a Mark of Fear

Austin

1900

Alpha LaRue Eberhart was born on August 5, 1867, in Albion, Illinois, a small town northeast of Evanston, to Jeremiah Snyder Eberhart (1836–1921) and Emma Swift May (1839–1928).

Jeremiah had grown up on his family's farm on the Allegheny River in Pennsylvania. When called to the ministry in adolescence, he was sent to Cornell College in Iowa, where he became known for his intelligence and devotion to his studies. Cornell College had accepted women since its inception, and it was there that Jeremiah met his future bride, Emma Swift May. They married in 1864 and returned to Albion to make their home. Three years later, they brought into the world their only child, Alpha LaRue.

Itinerant ministry garnered meager earnings, and A.L.'s family moved regularly as Jeremiah served a string of towns across Iowa and Illinois. Eventually, he looked for a place where he could make more money and provide Emma and A.L. with a more stable home. They settled in an area on the southwest side of Chicago called Chicago Lawn. There, Jeremiah soon traded preaching for real estate while carrying on voluntary mission work in the inner city.

A.L.'s parents, both with full educations during a time when few, especially women, had such privilege, were committed to their son's schooling. A.L was expected to do well in class while also learning how to play piano and sing. He carried part-time jobs from the age of fourteen, when he became a chore boy on a farm. At fifteen, he found a job in a dry goods house. My grandfather did not go on to college, but by the age of twenty-one, he had saved enough money to open his Gent's Furnishings Store on the South Side of Chicago. It's there he became accustomed to fine clothing—and to selling. In a few years, he sold that enterprise and became a road salesman selling gloves for five years before settling in Springfield, Illinois, where he was offered a full-time job at the State House. In Springfield, he became known for his charisma and generosity toward others. Friends assumed he would pursue a life in politics.

Between 1888 and 1900, while A.L. came of age, the US experienced two major financial panics and one recession. In 1892, the New York state legislature passed a law mandating railroads to impose a maximum ten-hour workday for switchmen, and to significantly increase their wages. When the Lehigh Valley, Erie, and Buffalo Creek Railroads refused to obey these laws, their switchmen went on strike. That same year, forty-nine affiliated unions, including teamsters, meatpackers, and scalesmen, formed their own generalized strike. At the same time, New Orleans's natural gas and electrical grid failed, generating widespread panic. Construction businesses, street cleaning, manufacturing plants, and firefighting ground to a halt. The poor national economy appeared to have little impact on George Hormel as he founded his company in Austin, Minnesota. He made his first annual kill of 610 hogs that year.

In January 1893, ten days before Grover Cleveland became president and after a long period of financial over-extension, the Philadelphia and Reading Railroads went bankrupt. As perception of the US economy worsened, people rushed to collect their cash, causing runs on banks, leading to the failure of 15,000 companies and 500 banks, many of them in the Midwest and West. Previously secure middle-class families were suddenly unable to make their mortgage obligations, and many walked away from their newly built Victorian homes. Hence, the term "haunted house" became associated with Victorians, perhaps like the one my father and Rog Catherwood sought to find in the summer of 1919.

Between the Panic of 1893 and the Panic of 1896, the US was only out of recession for six months. Both panics brought high unemployment. In 1897, after a long string of over-investing in an unprofitable railroad company, the National Bank of Illinois failed. It was federal examiners who discovered this overextension, the largest failure in the country which led to many closures of smaller Chicago banks. Along with these closures came high-profile banker suicides, which terrified remaining executives who expected their enterprises might be next up for examination. George Hormel would later claim that he barely survived the Panic of 1896 but did so by selling better product than his competitors, thereby capturing what remained of the market for meat.

It was against this tough economic backdrop that George reached out to my grandfather in 1901 and asked him to take a chance on his little meatpacking company in Austin.

LENA LOWENSTEIN WAS BORN ON NOVEMBER 25, 1874, in Wilmington, Illinois (now Patterson). The family would later move to White Hall, a prosperous and growing small city of under 2,000 residents located two hundred and sixty miles from Chicago.

Lena was the tenth-born in a family of eleven children. Her father, William Isidor Lowenstein, and her mother, Elizabeth Ann Ghormley, were both born in 1833, and had each emigrated from Germany. Isidor, called Isaac, made the cross-Atlantic voyage on his own at the age of seventeen. He first lived with an aunt in Philadelphia to learn English. At eighteen, he purchased a wholesale collection of dry goods and set off traveling north to Boston and south to Tennessee, selling his wares. Eventually, he made enough money to find his way to Illinois, where he met and married Elizabeth Ann Ghormley.

Later, in the 1940s, Lena's older sister Louise wrote to my father that a family helper called in to assist Elizabeth—who was chronically ill, in no small part due to having born eleven children—announced Lena's birth to her older siblings by telling them a new baby had been found in the woodpile. Perhaps it was a joke, perhaps just an old-fashioned way of announcing a baby, but a crush of siblings rushed to the pile to see if they could find any more.

Baby Lena's picture would be the first photograph taken in America of someone in the Lowenstein family, but only due to the quick thinking of her oldest brother, Polk, then fifteen, who scooped up his infant sister and took her to a photographer who was passing through town. Bright-eyed and energetic, Lena threw her arms into the air to greet the photographer's flash.

Young Lena grew up with an affable disposition and a mind of her own. If an older brother annoyed her, she'd grab him with both hands and kick him in the shins. Girls were expected to wear their hair long, but Lena insisted on cutting hers short. *You can't imagine what an occasion that was in those times*, Louise would later write to my father.

The Lowenstein family brought their German values with them to this country. Both girls and boys were expected to complete a full education, including learning proper elocution and the musical arts. Through her school years, Lena, especially, would become known for her beautiful singing voice, one my cousin El would inherit. Lena would tell her siblings she'd developed her voice by sitting next to her open bedroom window in White Hall, imitating birds.

From a young age, Lena believed in taking on any challenge she met—and she expected to surmount each one. On her first day of school, her teacher asked the students to prepare a speech to perform the following week. Precocious and uninterested in delay, Lena marched to the front of the room, stepped up onto the platform, and delivered a coherent and persuasive oratory. Reading these stories from her sister Lou's letters to my father made me instantly fall in love with my grandmother; I only wished I'd inherited more of her spunk.

Lena grew into a petite young woman with a head of thick, dark curls and dark brows. She was considered the most beautiful daughter in the Lowenstein family. By the age of twenty, everyone expected she'd have found herself a man to marry.

IN 1897, A.L. EBERHART, THEN WORKING AT the State House in Springfield, lived in a rooming house across the hall from a contemporary named Mr. Buck. Buck was courting a young woman in White Hall, and one day he invited A.L. to join him for the weekend. Maybe, he said, they could find my grandfather a good match there.

As the men drove through While Hall the next Saturday morning, A.L. noticed a young woman leaning against a column on the wide veranda of a sturdy, white-painted, clapboard house, singing. Lena Lowenstein was attired in a tailored, white–dotted swiss dress that pinched her waistline and set off her dense curls, pulled back in a chignon.

"There's the girl I've been looking for," A.L. later claimed to have said to his friend.

Lena's attraction to A.L. was immediate, though she took her time to evaluate his potential as a suitor and future husband. Through A.L.'s many trips to White Hall over the next year, he got to know the Lowensteins. Lena was still mourning the death of her father two years earlier at the age of sixty-five, cause unknown. She had been particularly close to him. A.L. sought her hand in marriage, but Lena held him off as she coped with her grief.

Finally, Emma Eberhart invited Lena for a proper visit to the family home in Chicago. Her older sister Lou served as chaperone. Both young women evaluated the Eberharts as suitable for Lena, in part because they held similar values about education and its importance for both girls and boys.

Lena made it clear to her suitor that she'd rather live in Chicago than Springfield. Which meant A.L. had to find new work in a poor economy. The story goes that he made his way to the behemoth Swift & Company, pushed past its guards and into the private office of founder Gustavus Swift, and pleaded for a place in the company. So impressed with A.L.'s determination, Swift hired him on the spot to work in the plant's shipping department. There, A.L. wrote later, he *jostled barrels of meat and lard and tried to make [himself] useful.*

A.L. and Lena set a wedding date and were married on June 22, 1898, at the Lowenstein family home in White Hall. Her older brother Louis walked her into the parlor, where the ceilings and doors were festooned with pink ribbons and smilax. Potted plants rested on the floor, and the family's heirloom German candelabras were filled with wax tapers. What a bittersweet day it must have been for Lena, having lost her beloved father and found her husband. The local newspaper described her as *levelheaded, modest, and cultured*, and that she wore a white French nainsook dress with lace and ribbon trimmings. Her bouquet was made from lilies of the valley and ferns. A.L. sported a full dress suit and was accompanied by his first cousin.

A.L. presented Lena with a diamond brooch for her wedding gift, and A.L. was given a silver card case from George Hastings Swift—Gustavus Swift's son and friend of A.L.'s. The couple departed from White Hall on the 10:40 p.m. train for the Windy City on the evening of their wedding ceremony. Jeremiah and Emma Eberhart had given the couple a brick flat at 4313 Berkeley Avenue in northeast Chicago, and the newlyweds needed to get established there for A.L. to begin his new job.

Gustavus Swift quickly recognized A.L.'s prodigious ability to sell and advanced him in position five times during his first year of employment until he held the highest sales position in Swift's Chicago headquarters.

WITHIN ANOTHER YEAR, A.L.'S FORTUNE IMPROVED: Swift & Company relocated him to St. Paul, where he would head up Swift's growing sales offices.

Through the research I was doing on the Lowenstein side of my family, I learned—from a letter my father's younger sister, Elizabeth, wrote to him as an adult—that my great-grandfather Isaac served as a Confederate in the Civil War. This came as a shock. Isaac lived in Union country, and nothing in his politics suggested that he would support the Confederate cause. Story has it that his choice was pragmatic—a strong trait in the Lowenstein lineage. Isaac volunteered for the Confederacy because, as a father of three children and in a dismal economy, he believed he'd be less likely to see combat as a Confederate. This consideration proved prescient, as he was quickly captured by the Union army and held prisoner, thereby never seeing battle.

Being a prisoner was far from any expectation Isaac would have had when he decided to enlist. With no means of support through her husband's absence, Emma and their first three children grew close to starvation as he languished in jail. Isaac needed to do something to save his family. He landed on offering haircuts to fellow prisoners, making pennies for each one. Eventually, the pennies added to a dollar he could send home to his wife. Union jailers were well known for pilfering, however, so Isaac's pragmatism included cutting each dollar in half and sending one half to his wife. When he learned by mail that she'd received it, he sent the other half. He got around the pilfering and his family survived his incarceration and the Civil War, if barely.

I learned more unexpected details about Lena's family when my second cousin Jack Fishback, a grandson of Lena's older sister Louise, conducted extensive research of our genealogy and discovered that Lena's father and mother were both German Jews. While Isaac arrived in the US on his own, Emma arrived with her parents and siblings. But her mother and father left sisters and brothers and their children behind in Germany. Tragically, Lena's family who remained in Germany—my great-great-family members—were later murdered at Auschwitz.

The new knowledge of our Jewish heritage sent shock waves through my family, especially my father and his brother, Dryden, both of whom found the news difficult to assimilate.

My cousins and I found our parents' initial reactions small-minded and xenophobic, and thought it fascinating that we were one-quarter Jewish. It took months to process what it meant to know that we had family members who died at Auschwitz. My only consolation was that Grandmother Lena died too young, long before Hitler's rise in Germany, to know of the deaths of her family members.

It's hard to believe that Lena, as perceptive a woman as she was, didn't know about her Jewish heritage. Perhaps on arrival in the United States, both Isaac Lowenstein and Emma Ghormley could see that anti-Semitism was rampant and buried their heritage for self-protection. If Lena knew, I don't know if she told A.L.; or, if she did tell him, why the two kept it private from their children, unless they both agreed, if tragically, that their children would be safer for not knowing.

ACCORDING TO FAMILY RECORDS AND IN LATER descriptions of A.L. by George Hormel, my grandfather quickly learned the meatpacking business under Gustavus Swift while developing a reputation for *square dealing* with his customers. A.L. was erudite and charming. His tastes ranged from simple pleasures of time spent outdoors to the latest fine cigar, a hand-tailored suit, and a starched shirt collar. At Swift & Company, he became known as a kind and natural leader with an aptitude for coaching young salesmen to succeed. In an era of business tycoons and autocrats, A.L. was, my father said, a humanist, something with which industry journals agreed. He believed business success could only be won by caring for those who worked for you, regardless of their role, and he was widely admired by all employees at Swift for not showing singular favor to those in positions of power.

George Hormel's and my grandfather's different countenances would seem to have made for odd business partners—and it's to George's credit that he was willing to seek outside talent; that is something that not all CEOs, then or now, would have done. I like to believe that George needed not only my grandfather's sales and merchandising skills but also his even, congenial personality—not something George was known for. And A.L. would bring with him all he'd learned from the leading manufacturer of processed meats. His hiring would have been seen as an indication that Hormel meant business, that he intended to build something of significant value.

I don't know how Gustavus Swift felt about my grandfather leaving his employ, but it didn't affect the friendship my grandfather had with his son George, a friendship that would remain throughout his life and extend beyond A.L. to my father.

On May 28, 1901, A.L. accepted George Hormel's offer of employment. He would be paid an annual salary, yearly additions of company stock, and 10 percent of net profits per year. A floor for profits was set equal to his salary, and no ceiling was established. *I have this day tendered my resignation to Swift*, my grandfather wrote to his new boss, *and will advise you in the near future as to when I expect to report to you for work.*

In exchange for his move to Austin, A.L. was given the title of sales manager and corporate secretary of Geo. A. Hormel & Company, making him the sole non-family member of the Hormel company's board of directors. According to my family's stories, and colleagues of A.L.'s inside the company, he was brought in, in part, to ensure that

George Hormel had a suitable successor should anything befall him, or should he later retire.

With hundreds of small meatpacking companies going out of business between Chicago and South Dakota and most families across the US cutting back their discretionary spending on meat, maybe my grandfather was wooed by the opportunity to make a signature mark in this new venture, even if Austin and the Hormel company were still rough around the edges. What Austin had going for it was a good rail link, which A.L. knew how to exploit. Maybe, too, as my father would later speculate, A.L. considered the offer of a seat on the board, annual infusions of company stock, and 10 percent of net profits his bird in the hand. In a giant company like Swift's, his long-term prospects might not have been so clear.

I wonder, too, whether the wide-open spaces of southern Minnesota attracted him, as they had George Hormel. A.L. had spent his teenage summers working on remote horse and cattle ranches in the outback of Colorado. He loved sitting in a saddle and riding the range; he enjoyed being around livestock, and especially loved wild places, of which Minnesota had plenty.

AFTER ACCEPTING THE NEW OFFER, A.L. and Lena quickly set up their first home in Austin at 811 Kenwood Avenue. It was an accommodating wood-frame house with a gable window facing the street and a full veranda across the front. Photographs of that place show a rocking chair and hammock on the front porch, where the Eberharts communed with neighbors and, in the future, would watch their young children play.

One year after A.L. moved to Austin, President McKinley was assassinated and Teddy Roosevelt became president of the United States. Austin's population had grown to 5,037 residents and the Hormel company processed nearly 33,000 hogs that year, bringing in sales of $711,000—a 70 percent increase from the prior year. There was a boom afoot in the early years of the 1900s as thousands of settlers moved west and required goods of all kinds, including meats. Still, A.L.'s sales leadership was showing success.

Through the next dozen years, A.L. would open or expand Hormel branches in Duluth (1904), St. Paul (1905), St. Louis (1910), San Antonio (1911), Minneapolis (1912), and Chicago (1913), to be followed in ensuing years by ones in Waco, Providence, New York, and Boston, handily pitting the growing company against the giants of Armour and Swift. All the while, he maintained his close friendship with George Swift through an active correspondence and at industry conventions in Chicago and Boston. As A.L. helped to grow the Hormel company, it provided solid employment for hundreds of people and significantly raised the standard of living of Mower County, Minnesota.

7.

He Could Sell Refrigerators to Eskimos

Austin

1900

In 1902, Main Street in Austin was paved, and A.L.'s first child, Alpha Dryden Eberhart, was born. My father, Richard Ghormley Eberhart, followed in 1904. Establishing sales branches and overseeing work at the packing plant kept A.L. busy, whether he was in Austin or traveling to other cities. Lena tended to the Eberhart home on Kenwood Avenue and the needs of her growing family.

The year my father was born, the meatpackers union in Chicago went on strike—which Swift and Armour proceeded to break. During this time, Upton Sinclair, a self-proclaimed socialist from a wealthy family in Virginia, was in Chicago doing research for a novel he was writing about the plight of the poor, set in the meatpacking industry. As he got to know many of the striking workers and their families, he learned of men with advanced skin diseases from working in the meat pickling rooms, men who'd lost fingers from knife accidents on the assembly lines that kept being sped up, men crippled by heaving hundred-pound hunks of animal carcasses from floor to floor. He discovered that the primitive bathrooms available to these workers provided no soap or water, and there were no clean lunchrooms where workers could eat.

The next year, his seminal novel *The Jungle*—intended as a call to action about the plight of the poor and their treatment in rapidly growing factories and cities—was published to public acclaim. By this time, the beginning of the new century, public rebuke of large corporations was on the rise, with growing distaste for the likes of Standard Oil and U.S. Steel, along with the meatpacking companies of Armour and Swift, all of them assumed to be practicing business unfairly and treating workers as near slaves. Sinclair and others hoped to promote public ownership of these industries—but companies ignored the critique, claiming their right to do business as they saw fit.

The Jungle was a book of fiction but read as true as nonfiction, and it became an instant international best seller, published in seventeen languages. In it, Chicago meatpacking houses were portrayed as places of dark and dangerous work where employees stood on floors covered in blood, scrap, and fetid water. Through their days, immigrants from Poland, Lithuania, and Slovakia experienced inadequate airflow, extreme heat in summer, and no heat in winter. Workers included men, women, and children whose daytime accommodations were as bad as the crowded tenements and rented rooms they slept in at night next to the stockyards and Chicago dumps. If Sinclair was upset that the public's outcry focused more on filth in meatpacking plants than on the workers themselves, his book still moved a nation.

By that time, four major meatpacking companies had bought out most of the smaller ones, allowing themselves to dictate prices to retail customers and what they paid for feed, cattle, and hogs. It was meatpackers, especially Swift, who were developing early assembly lines, and hastening the work employees had to do by designating dozens of specialized jobs—positions like "ripper," "leg breaker," "gutter," and "knocker." In my research, I've learned many of these titles still exist. No longer did a man look at an entire hog, perhaps even consider it a sentient being necessarily sacrificed for his nutrition; now workers dismembered bloody carcasses that circulated in huge rooms on hooks at such speed that they could barely keep up. Most of the meat was used for wholesale or retail markets, while bones, fat, organs, and other scraps were turned into soap and fertilizer. In meatpacking parlance, the companies tried to use "everything but the squeal."

President Roosevelt had long favored large enterprises for their efficiency and scale, but in response to a civic outcry about the nation's meat supply, he admitted that in meatpacking plants, *there is filth on the floor, and it must be scraped up with the muckrake.*

The White House was inundated with letters from outraged Americans, and Roosevelt was forced to rush out the country's first law regulating food and drugs. Signed on June 30, 1906, the Pure Food and Drugs Act regulated food additives and monitored misleading labeling, alongside the Meat Inspection Act. These acts would eventually lead to the formation of the Federal Drug Administration (FDA) we know today.

The new requirements of these acts led many small meatpackers to fail, as they were unable to comply with the increase in regulations covering packinghouses. George Hormel, however, was able to make the necessary changes and demanded absolute adherence to the law. When the newly trained federal agents Roosevelt dispatched westward to examine every plant in the country arrived in Austin to tour the Hormel plant, they were singularly impressed with its cleanliness and operations; in fact, the *Austin Herald* quoted federal agents as saying the company was *among the most perfect in the country from sanitary and inspection standpoints.*

With that endorsement, Geo. A. Hormel & Company's reputation grew fast, garnering favor among housewives across the country. The increasing population throughout the Midwest and the newly instituted regulations for meat handling led to greater demand for Hormel products, and A.L. harnessed his sales strategy to that trajectory, quickly expanding sales branches across the country.

In 1904, the year my father was born, A.L. opened his first new sales office, in Duluth (some sources say it was in 1908 but family letters suggest 1904). Duluth was the perfect choice for escalating the delivery of processed meats to more substantial markets, both east and west. A drive to Duluth, located 250 miles north of Austin, could take six hours, but A.L. chose it for its port, the busiest in the country at the time. With its position on Lake Superior, the gross tonnage of goods it moved surpassed even New York City. Lake vessels carried iron ore through Duluth to Illinois and Ohio for refining and processing. The city was growing rapidly, boasting ten newspapers, six banks, and more millionaires per capita than anywhere in the United States. Anticipating the arrival of U.S. Steel's new $5 million plant that year, the city was considered progressive for its time.

Key to growth in Duluth was recruiting and training the right sales office staff—from salesmen to stenographers and clerks. A.L. needed to divvy up territories and accurately account for salesmen's revenue and expenses, while following the differing laws of each state in which the company did business. George Hormel and my grandfather both knew they had the better-quality animals, the better product, and the more innovative cuts than Swift and Armour. It was just up to A.L. to sell them. An expressed goal was to procure the accounts of every hotel in the city, so travelers through Duluth would only find Hormel meats to eat.

The original province of the Ojibwe, this was a place of expansive land and big water, settled by Scandinavian immigrants who had established a modern, cosmopolitan city. By the time my grandfather arrived, the Minnesota rail system had built out an effective overlapping grid connecting all parts of the state. From Duluth, any commodity could be transported to Minneapolis and Chicago. From Chicago, goods could go anywhere in the world, by water or by rail. Opening the Duluth branch was the modern equivalent of plugging Hormel's small Austin meat factory into the World Wide Web. The office was immediately successful.

I imagine my grandfather enjoying a leisurely walk along the waterfront on Lake Superior at the end of a long day, scouting barges and tankers, chatting with dockwollapers and tugboat captains. Maybe he stayed at the Spalding Hotel on Superior Street, an eight-story redbrick and terra-cotta building, capped with a mansard roof, and round towers on its corners. Paneling made from quarter-sawn oak graced its inside walls, its ladies' writing room provided a quiet space for women to gather in private, and its grand lobby boasted a handsome bar. I like to think of A.L. meeting potential salesmen there and welcoming a steady stream of bankers and financiers, real estate agents, industrialists, and sales candidates. I like to think of him drinking a brandy where Presidents Truman and Roosevelt had. He would certainly have dined on the hotel's signature planked white fish while trying to sell the chef on Hormel chops. Maybe Duluth brought him back to memories of his adolescence in Chicago when he walked along the shore of Lake Michigan.

Letters he mailed home to Lena described his excitement. On behalf of George Hormel, he was proud of the innovative upstart company making waves in southern Minnesota. At the end of each long day, he penned his nightly letter to Lena, usually beginning with, *Dear one, my news today is . . .* and always ending with, *Devotedly, your husband, A.L. Eberhart.*

Astute, perceptive, and fond of people, A.L. enjoyed looking a prospect in the eye and, if satisfied with the integrity of the relationship and the price established, closing a deal. The Hormel company's newsletter, *Squeal*, would later call him a "sales genius." George Hormel would write that A.L. could probably *sell refrigerators to Eskimos.*

A.L.'s relationships with business associates naturally turned into warm friendships. He invited his customers for golf matches and camping trips. He took them hunting and fishing in the woods and on the lakes of northern Minnesota. This has long been the way men have done business—combining industry conversation with recreation in relaxed spaces. I'm sure these outings helped cement his network of colleagues while gaining him the reputation he deserved, for being not only effective in business but also fun to be with. While George Hormel attended to the minutiae of building out his administration, A.L. quickly became the face of the company.

8.

On My Own

Austin

1997

It's been two years since El and I were in Austin, and this time I'm back with Michael, who came into my life as a lovely surprise when I was forty. We both owned our own companies, easily revealed our family skeletons and shared how we'd been coming to terms with them. Mostly, we got to know each other by talking a lot, eating out, and dancing. Michael's mother came from Minnesota, so he was eager to accompany me on this trip.

Driving south from the airport in Minneapolis, we make a quick jog west to Owatonna, where I lived in the summer of 1968—the place where I witnessed little Maria's cotton dress scorching with flame.

"I'm curious what thirty years has done to the town," I say to Michael as he navigates with a paper map.

"Looks like it's only about a half hour out of our way."

"How 'bout we find lunch there and then head to Austin?" I suggest.

We find the Salvation Army building, the site of our hastily set-up home base back in 1968. Then, it was an old lumberyard that we molded to our purposes—fitting in a makeshift kitchen with folding tables for dining and converting two lumber bays to girls' and boys' bunk rooms. Today, the building is still here, but it's been converted into rental storage. No one's around and the doors are locked, but it's still good to see the old place where I spent that especially memorable summer.

"I wonder if I can find the Summers' house," I say while Michael and I sit in the park and he peruses a free newspaper to see where to find lunch.

Aside from working in the Mexican migrant camp at the Owatonna Canning Company that summer, our group scoured and painted the two-story clapboard house of an impoverished and intellectually disabled couple with six young children. I'd walked there from the warehouse many times, so I'm able to find the street by feel. Now it's a well-kept home with a mowed front lawn edged in flowering hydrangeas. A small addition has been attached to one side, creating a better entryway than the one I remember. With its corner position on a sunny street, the home has good bones, something like a small New England colonial. Memories of the Summers family flood in as I stare at the house.

"The place was squalid," I tell Michael. "We wrapped bandanas around our faces to breathe, the smell of urine was so strong. There was a pail of diapers overflowing on the first floor. With maggots."

He winces.

"I'd seen poverty but never that bad." I shake my head. "There were twenty churches in this town, but it took nineteen teenagers from far away to bring attention to this family."

Michael and I walk around the corner to get a different angle on the house, and from there we can just make out the backyard. No one is around.

"On that wall there was this dark stain running down to the ground from the second-floor window. We couldn't figure out why; there wasn't any sign of leaking upstairs. Then Andrew and I—he was this big, beautiful Latino kid from Philly—we were cleaning up the yard mess to set up ladders for scraping and painting, and we looked up to see one of the littler kids push his butt out the screenless window and pee against the wall."

Michael laughs.

"It was quite a sight," I say, chuckling with him. "The toilet was backed up, so I guess they got creative."

That summer of my adolescence opened my eyes to the landscape of the Midwest and to how unfair life is— that some of us have so much and others so little. Each evening my peers and I brought our indignation to our group leaders and thrashed through our anger and passion in the hot, windowless lumberyard late into the night. It was there that I started looking at things through the lens of systems—governmental, religious, corporate, familial—and how power in systems was concentrated at the top, with positions usually held by men, be they presidents, priests, CEOs, or fathers.

"A few months later, back in New Hampshire, full of energy to change the world, Dad molested me. At the party for Anne Sexton, right after she'd won her Pulitzer Prize."

I look at Michael, who knows the story but may understand the context for the trauma better now.

"All that passion just got squashed," I say. "Sometimes it feels almost intentional, as if to dampen my emerging womanhood just as it was taking off. I just went inward in shame."

Michael gathers me in his arms.

"I told no one. Took years before I did," I say, pressing my face into his shoulder. "I felt like I'd become detached from myself. Out here, I was an equal member of a summer family; I returned home to be a subservient one in my own."

We walk back to the front of the house.

"I'm sad for the passionate young woman I left behind."

Michael steers me back to the car. "It's gotta be hard to be here," he says.

"Yeah, but it's good to find this house, and to remember what I was like before what happened at home." I lean against the car door. "And how my work with companies had its genesis here, in those long conversations about systems. I guess I work with CEOs because they have the power to change them—and I can ensure that women's voices are included in their decisions, as we're the ones who so often see what needs to change."

AFTER A QUICK CHANGE OF CLOTHES AT OUR hotel in Austin, Michael and I meet up with Mike and Barb Ruzek for an early dinner at the new Applebee's, to be followed by the Friday night high school football game.

Mike's an insurance guy who El and I first met during our visit to Austin in 1995 and we've stayed in touch since then. Born and raised in Austin, he founded the Austin High School Alumni and Friends Association and is a champion of all things Austin. Like Betty Catherwood, he seems to know every person in town. I'm looking forward to having him meet Michael, for whom Mike has graciously found a golfing partner for tomorrow, so I can be free to do my research.

"Welcome back," he says as we settle into our generously sized booth.

Michael enjoys football, so he and Mike fall into sports banter over their favorite teams during dinner. From the start, one thing I loved about Michael was how he could talk to anyone. Though not extroverted by nature, he's a good listener and easy conversationalist—a skill he employs regularly both on the golf course and in the business he owns and runs.

THE FOOTBALL STADIUM PARKING LOT IS PACKED with cars. We arrive just in time to watch the players be introduced and get set for the kickoff. Every inch of two concrete bleachers on both sides of the field is filled with fans: Austin Packers fans on one side, Albert Lea visitors on the other. The stadium was built as a WPA project in the 1930s and for years was considered one of the finest football stadiums in Minnesota. The energy here—and this is a high school game—rivals what we feel at Red Sox games in Boston. It's electric.

The field lines are freshly painted. The bright bulbs on the tall light stands make clear every inch of the ground. Each Packer bursts onto the playing field to thunderous applause (it seems four thousand fans stomping their feet can make a lot of noise). The boys' signature red-and-white uniforms make for an early Christmas display on the emerald field. Mike has situated us at the fifty-yard line, about ten rows up from the grass, providing a grand view of the spectacle.

Mike and Michael evaluate the plays on the field while I scan the social scene and chat with Barb, a psychiatric nurse at St. Mary's Hospital in Rochester, Minnesota. Little kids toss popcorn into each other's mouths. Two teenagers roam the sidelines dressed in jeans, their arms around each other, the girl wearing a letterman jacket, likely his. She occasionally tosses her shoulder-length blond hair alluringly, though she's already won the boy. I'm brought back to my last two years in high school, after being molested and as the Vietnam War escalated from 1967 to 1969. I had no interest in sports and was intimidated by the in-crowd with their easy hookups, their we're-together-forever relationships. Now, I wonder if I lost out on something. Back then, it never occurred to me that anyone else in my town had been assaulted by a family member. It wouldn't be until years later, after #MeToo, that I would learn that I was not the only one in my class who had been. If only we'd known in 1968.

I glance at Michael and Mike, who are leaning forward and ping-ponging critiques back and forth about the game.

"Mike, have I told you my father quarterbacked this team in 1920?" I ask. "Lena and A.L. must have stood close to here watching his games."

"Isn't that something," Mike says.

"Seventy-five years ago."

"A long time," he replies.

"This was the perfect thing to do tonight," Michael says.

It's so American, I think to myself.

A pleasant evening with nice people, surrounded by a proud community showing off its best. What's not to love about Austin?

SATURDAY MORNING, MIKE'S FRIEND PICKS UP Michael at our hotel and takes him to the Austin Country Club, leaving me with our rental car.

The Club was founded in 1919 as a three-hole course with sand traps. George Hormel was its founder and first president. In 1920, the course was expanded to nine holes and became known as the shortest in the US. The following summer of 1921, the new clubhouse opened and golfers navigated their expanded course around the hazard of Dobbins Creek snaking through the fairways. Meanwhile, Hormel workers in town wondered if they'd be able to keep their jobs as Ransome Thomson was put behind bars for his million-dollar-plus embezzlement.

Now the course is beautifully cooled by large maple and oak trees.

IT'S A SHORT DRIVE TO THE MOWER COUNTY Historical Society, housed next to the county fair buildings. I'm looking for Ella Marie Lausen, a volunteer who Mike told me over dinner is *the* person to see about Austin and Mower County history. He's arranged for her to meet me while Michael plays golf.

I find her seated behind a wooden desk. She rises and extends a warm handshake. We share a small, compact physique, but her hair is gray and I'd wager she's around seventy to my forty-seven. Her bright blue eyes and open face convey an immediate trust. Her steps are short and quick, reminding me of my mom, who was always on the go. She shows none of the defensiveness of V., the Hormel archivist with whom El and I met at the Spam Museum.

The historical society was formed in 1947, following that year's county fair honoring all farmers in Mower County who had worked the land and paid taxes for fifty-plus years. Fifty-two men and women were celebrated, and a group of them dedicated themselves to preserving important agricultural and civic history by instituting this group. Since then, multiple historic buildings—a log cabin, a church, an old Hormel shed, and a blacksmith shop—have been moved to the site. There's a pioneer home with a potbelly stove, a barn housing a vintage tractor, a small wooden schoolhouse where kids come to see how their forebears learned. It's an extensive hodgepodge of buildings and artifacts, including a Sherman tank, but its central administration is held in a simple one-story office with wooden columns holding up its overhanging roof.

I learn that Ella Marie's family members were Mower County farmers, probably among the ones celebrated in 1947. She's retired from a thirty-year teaching career in Austin, and has served on the county fair board for years.

When I ask about her teaching career, she tells me she taught mostly on the east side of Austin, the side called Dutch Town.

"I loved the children—and their families," she says. "I heard stories of the Thomson embezzlement and I knew your grandfather's name, of course."

"Why was it called Dutch Town?" I ask.

"Austin was full of Dutch immigrants, and most lived on that side of the railroad. They were the early Hormel workers."

Mike's put me in good hands, I think.

"Have you read George Hormel's autobiography?" she asks. "It was never published, but it has quite a lot of information."

I'm immediately intrigued. I didn't know it existed.

"We have a copy. You'll read about your grandfather. Mr. Hormel writes that letting him go was one of the hardest things he ever had to do."

I snicker.

"That's how he describes it," she says.

I worry I've offended her. "I'd like to read that," I say quickly.

Ella Marie turns toward a back room and returns with a simply bound book called *The Open Road*. Several hundred pages of manuscript, it was typed out on eight-by-eleven paper, back-to-back. She points out the chapters I should read.

"Can I get a copy of the book?" I ask.

"Not really," she says. "It's never been published, so it's not for sale. The Hormel family gave a copy to the public library, and we have one here. I can copy specific pages if you'd like."

She points me to a table and chair, and I'm grateful for a chance to peruse the book. After skimming through the introduction and table of contents, I head to later chapters covering the era of my grandfather's involvement with the company. George writes that he didn't blame my grandfather for the stealing, which makes me suspect of V.'s suggestion that he was in cahoots, but adds that he questioned my grandfather's loyalties.

Loyalties? I've never heard that A.L. was disloyal to anyone or any job.

I'm intrigued by George Hormel's voice as he writes about his early years in Toledo and the company's beginnings. He sounds reasonable, not at all like the brute I've heard described. But he also sounds like a man might toward the end of his career, putting down his version of what happened for generations after him. On the other hand, given that it was written with no expectation of publication, I take it for fairly accurate.

As Knowles Dougherty suggested when El and I met him, George does come across as obsessed with success. And glad to have earned it.

I lift my head and stare out the window at a large tree adjacent to the office. Its branches and leaves shade the building and give my eyes a place to rest. I think about the meaning of success in my family. For my father, it seemed to be about the company you kept, the people you knew, the awards you won, the prestige you were held in. My brother and I were measured against neighbor kids when we stood flat-footed against the doorframe of our kitchen, a book on our heads to verify our height. To be taller was to succeed, to have grown up, so I'd raise my heels off the floor, trying not to wobble. I wonder, now, how much of my father's literary drive came from trying to measure up to A.L.'s *six feet of manhood*. And did A.L. measure his own success by sales, sales branches, and the revenue he generated for the Hormel company? Or was it by the magnificent estate he built and the comfort it provided his family?

I go back to reading. An hour passes while I devour this book, jotting down notes on George Hormel. I find his background intriguing; he seems smart as a manager and faithful to the cause of his company. I ask Ella Marie to make copies of two chapters.

"Have you been to LeRoy?" she asks on her return.

"No. I've heard of it. I read about it in Richard Dougherty's books."

LeRoy was the site of Cy Thomson's Oak Dale Farms and Amusement Park, the primary bucket for the money he embezzled.

"It's about an hour's drive from here," she says. "I could take you tomorrow."

I tally whether Michael and I have time to fit this in and realize we don't. "I would love to go, but I'm afraid it's not in the cards for this trip. Hopefully next time!"

She nods. "Back when Thomson built his park, it would have taken two or three times that by car. Some rode their horses or went in horse-drawn carriages. The train might have gotten you there in an hour if it was on time and if you had money for a ticket."

What's now an hour's drive on a smooth highway was in 1920 a place the average person couldn't have visited regularly. Maybe that distance shielded Cy's extravagances from any observing eyes at the Hormel company in Austin. Later, I'll learn he built three farms, one of them in Austin, along with a fine home, and still no one thought he was stealing money.

"There's not much left of what he built," Ella Marie tells me, "but someday you should go. I've collected some photographs. Just a minute."

She brings me a pile of black-and-white and sepia-toned photographs. Her eyes glisten like flecks of gold once panned from the Cedar River. I can tell she's invested in my search, and I'm grateful. There's no one else here, so we're free to talk across the room.

She turns to me, shoulders forward, and hands me a copy of *Mill on the Willow: A History of Mower County*. It is full of photographs, along with a four-hundred-page story—who

knew so much could be said in photographs about flat, endless land? Ella Marie points to a drawing of Oak Dale Farms, which shows a different version from the few images I saw in the Dougherty books. The expanse of Cy's campus is clearer. A photograph of the parking lot shows five hundred black cars—mostly Fords, I'm guessing—lined up across multiple fields, as they were at Friday's football game. I have to think Oak Dale's customers were wealthy enough to own these cars and had the time and inclination to drive to LeRoy. My lips squinch as I slide my finger over the photos. These images match the stories I've heard from Dad. This great land of hardworking and adventurous immigrants. The pictures draw me in even more than George Hormel's words.

"Would you have a map of the county?" I ask. "I'd love to see what the distance looks like and how the roads were laid out between Austin and LeRoy."

She brings me a map and lays it out on the table. As we talk about the past, I feel our kinship growing. Ella Marie is a natural history buff with as many questions as I have about what happened to my grandfather, and she's not an unequivocal fan of George Hormel.

On her old map of Mower County, I see LeRoy and Austin in a straight line, with Cresco to the south and Blooming Prairie to the north. Blooming Prairie was the site for Cy Thomson's second farm, the one he filled with Duroc hogs. She points to the Red Cedar River, separating the east side of Austin—where she taught, the factory was located, and most of the Hormel workers lived—from the west side, where my father's family lived. The east side was more Democratic; the west side leaned Republican.

"This was Whispering Pines." She points to my grandfather's livestock ranch, just north of downtown Austin. "My grandfather was about the same age as George Hormel. And he had a farm here." She indicates the spot with her finger. "It's where I still live."

"Are your parents still alive?" I ask cautiously.

"No, they've passed."

Ella Marie tells me about 4-H and county fairs, judging animals, what it would have cost to buy a good Holstein. Pictures form in my mind. Around 1919, when A.L. bought his ranch at Whispering Pines and founded the Minnesota Holstein Company, he began to raise the prize-winning cows my cousins and I heard about as kids. Each cow had a name as long as a Faulkner sentence, which made them sound like British royalty.

Ella Marie points out how close Cy's second farm in Blooming Prairie was to A.L.'s Whispering Pines. It's easier to see how he and my grandfather weren't only colleagues at the Hormel factory but also neighboring landowners and investors in livestock. The inferences come on fast.

"Your grandfather was a serious investor," Ella Marie says. "He took a lot of pride in his herd. Most of the big prizes at county and state fairs went to his company."

She shows me a newspaper photo of Whispering Pines.

DAIRY FARMSTEAD — The large block-tile barn on the old Minnesota Holstein Farm has been an Austin landmark since the 1920s. The farm, then owned by A. L. Eberhart, a Hormel Co. official, was sold by Harold Westby to Joe West, Charles City, Iowa dairyman.

"I believe he even entered cattle in national livestock fairs in New York City," she adds.

Did A.L. invest in livestock and breeding to make more money? It certainly coincides with the time he took on the support of his aging parents—moving them to Austin, where they lived in a cottage on his property—and his three growing children moving toward adolescence. Or did he do it for the love of cattle ranches he'd developed during his summers in Colorado? Or was he thumbing his nose at his boss, suggesting he could build his own empire?

"While your grandfather was raising Holsteins," Ella Marie continues, "Cy Thomson was raising chickens and Duroc hogs."

She lays out a photograph of Cy's prize-winning chickens. They just look like chickens to me, but she tells me they were treated like queens. Cy built a specially designed chicken barn outfitted with state-of-the-art air filtering, along with dozens of high windows for natural light. Modern for its time. Ella Marie tells me that people judge character out here by the livestock they keep. Maybe it was natural for my grandfather to take part in this deeply embedded culture.

"Mr. Hormel, your grandfather, and Cy Thomson—all three wanted the best animals and each was admired for their herds."

"So, all three set their sights on animals—ones they could buy, win prizes for, make money from, or make into food," I muse. "This makes sense."

Ella Marie nods, setting her gray locks to bounce. I'm her pupil. She's helping me see that these men had big ambitions—that all three wanted to succeed.

"Didn't A.L. have a farm manager running his ranch?" I ask, recalling things I've heard from my dad. "Maybe others did the work, and he didn't spend that much time at it?" I'm bargaining with the idea that A.L. could have been "disloyal" to his work for the Hormel company.

"Yes, his foreman and his farmhands," she says. "But he would have been integrally involved in decisions. Back then, we didn't have absentee investors."

"Do you think my grandfather and Cy Thomson were friends?"

I've not mouthed these words to anyone other than El. It feels forbidden. My father looms in my mind for hinting at this line of inquiry.

"I'd dare say they must have been," she confirms. "They were social, both generous. Went to the same church. Held upper jobs at the company. They were in the same breeding circles. They were both admired throughout the state and beyond."

I tuck this news away. Dad used to tell me that growing up in Austin was like growing up in a small town—his family knew everyone and everyone knew them. And yet this is the first time I've heard anyone with knowledge of the people and place of that time speak so directly about a possible friendship between my grandfather and Cy Thomson.

I wonder if my father never suggested this because he didn't want to see that kind of connection.

Ella Marie is blowing open the doors on family myths we've safeguarded, inviting me to look inside. I glance at the clock; I've got another hour before Michael will be waiting at the golf course. I don't want to keep Ella Marie much longer, but I also don't want her to stop—and anyway, she's got more.

She presents me with another stack of newspaper clippings, ones she collected in anticipation of my arrival, along with pamphlets about Holsteins and records of prizes won by A.L. I paw through them like a kid rifling through jigsaw puzzle pieces. I have no idea how all the specks of information will fit together, but I'm determined to figure it out.

Periodically, I lift my head to ask Ella Marie a question.

"What do you think of the fact that my grandfather was fired?" I ask her.

"I never heard he was involved in the stealing," she says. "He was highly respected."

Ella Marie was born in 1922, so anything she's heard could be hearsay. Still, she is honest and transparent, a teacher. I don't think she'd say this if it wasn't something she'd heard from others who knew.

She repeats, "It's hard to believe that he'd be involved in any way in the stealing."

"But no one believed Cy Thomson could have done it either," I say. "He was respected and loved too."

She nods. "But your grandfather and Cy Thomson were cut from very different cloth."

I let that sink in. "From what I've read in A.L.'s letters, he was very close with meat executives, breeders, and brokers across the country. It was part of his job to create and maintain these relationships. I think Hormel probably hired him, in part, for those relations. His friends stayed with him through and after he left Austin and Hormel."

"We know he had strong friendships," she concurs. She's careful with her words but seems to be enjoying being encouraged to share her opinions.

I look at the clock again. Time to collect Michael. "I need to go," I tell Ella Marie, "and I don't want to hold you up any longer. But thank you. You've been *so* helpful."

"I've enjoyed it," she says.

I walk over to look her in the eye. "I want to know what my grandfather did," I say firmly, "even if it was wrong. I've worked with a lot of executive men, and I see them all in shades of gray. Their great strengths can be their undoing."

She nods in agreement. "Even after the embezzlement was discovered, there were a lot of people who continued to love Thomson. Some struggled to believe he could have done it. Many thought someone else in the company did it and he was their scapegoat. Most thought he'd curried more benefit to this place than trouble."

Her words come at me askew, the way the sun comes through a window at an angle, catching your eye and causing you to turn to avoid it.

"What I heard was that Mr. Hormel only cared about one thing," she adds. "Really, all he cared about was his money."

"Makes sense, maybe, since he grew up with none? Knowles Dougherty told me what he cared about most was to succeed, but success in business often equates to money."

"They were the same." She nods. "That's what I heard. George A. came from very little. And he made a lot. By any measure, he was a success. It must have been a terrible blow to have a trustworthy employee betray him like Cy Thomson did."

"Did you hear Hormel was basically a caring boss or more of a brute?"

Ella Marie rubs the back of her neck. "He was known as very demanding. Despite what comes across in his autobiography, he expected a lot from people. He made impulsive decisions. He wasn't easy to work for. Many still think your grandfather was wronged."

I'm writing down notes as quickly as I can. I'm not an investigative journalist, but I've interviewed a lot of people in my work and I know what to ask. I wonder if George's confession about his difficulty in letting my grandfather go was authentic. Did the decision haunt him? Was it an impulsive move, one he regretted?

Whatever the truth, he never changed his mind or shouldered any blame—not publicly, anyway—just as A.L. had known he wouldn't, and had written to George Swift.

I need to get to the golf course, but Ella Marie is telling me things I want to think about—especially that Cy and A.L. had to be friends, and that many people still think A.L. was wronged.

"Can you come back tomorrow?" she asks. "I should have more things for you."

"I think so," I say—but I stop short of committing. Michael and I need to sort out our priorities for Sunday morning before we head back to the airport. And honestly, I'm full-up with information and not sure how much more I can process.

Seeing me hesitate, she says, "I can make copies. Could we meet at eleven and you could pick them up?"

"Perfect," I say. "We'll be on our way to the airport. Would it be okay if I send you more questions if I have them?"

"Of course."

"I'll email you."

"Oh, no." Ella Marie laughs, shaking her head. "I don't use email. We'll just write."

I smile, enjoying this new, older friend with whom I suspect I will share correspondence in the future. I reach my hand out to shake hers before leaving.

"Goodbye for now," she says as I head out the door.

9.

Musings near a Putting Green

Austin

1997

Persistent questions and new evidence from my morning with Ella Marie rumble through my brain as I drive to the country club to pick up Michael. I'm irritated. Irritated for not being able to let go of this story, and then driven by what irritates me about it. I feel the grief and loss of not ever getting to know my grandparents, people I first came to love as a kid through my father's stories and now have come to love even more after reading their letters. I want them to be as they've been described to me, as they seem in their correspondence, then fear I'll learn something that will force me to question them. I'm the one turning over these stones; no one's forcing me, and yet I keep doing so.

There's no evidence of Michael as I park our car at the country club, which means he's been delayed on the course. Not unusual for a golf outing. I'm glad for a break from the mental stimulation Ella Marie has provided. Dates and times, places and pictures, livestock sales, old-fashioned Fords, mansions, ranches—they buzz like frenzied gnats in my head. I need to move details or get above them to see whatever it is I'm looking for. I trust the facts will sort themselves out; it's the emotional knocking about that's gotten to me. The new-to-me potential imperfections of my grandfather float in my mind like flotsam on an ocean's surface. Most top executives I've known don't just get fired for nothing.

I find a bench under a maple tree and slow my breath. A breeze, tender and welcome, heads up the fairway and cools my face. The leaves rustle above me. When contemplating complicated information, I much prefer to be outside. Better still to be outside and moving—on my feet, my bike, my skis; those are my preferred vehicles for thinking. This bench will have to do.

I mine my morning notes, inking in the missing halves of sentences, circling quotations, bulleting key points. Is it possible my father's story about George Hormel intending A.L. to be his successor wasn't true? From scanning two chapters of George's autobiography, I now know his only heir, Jay, was nine years old in 1901 when George hired A.L.—how could he promise my grandfather successorship when he didn't know if his own son might want the job? Wouldn't he have wanted to pass the family company on to his only child? Or could his intention have been only pragmatic—if anything should happen to him, he'd have installed a capable man who would carry the company on? CEOs make promises to prospective hires that they mean at the time but don't, or can't, always keep. Situations change. They change their minds.

A western meadowlark—identifiable because Michael showed me one earlier today—pecks at something on the ground next to my bench. Its breast carries a deep V; its throat and chest are the color of egg yolk. Its chirp is a set of long notes with a surprise wiggle at the end, like a flutist's quick coda. It seems late for this bird to be migrating to Oklahoma for winter.

Chewing on this conundrum about when it's time to leave a place and when it's time to stay, human or ornithological, I think back thirteen years to 1984, when I was promised a CEO job and then not given it. Pre-consulting career, I was executive director of a regional community health agency operating near a prominent medical center, and one of our key programs was a thriving visiting nurse service (VNA). Back then, nearly every town in New England had one, made up of trained nurses who could support older patients in their homes after hospitalization. There were eight VNAs in our corner of New Hampshire and Vermont, and the one I worked for was the largest by four times. Each agency received discharge referrals from the medical center. Each had its own intake procedures. Whereas the other seven were hard-pressed to do anything more than basic nursing care, ours could handle complicated in-home oxygen and feeding tubes. Each agency was governed by its own board and retained its own executive director and staff. Ours had been broadening its funding base; by 1984 we'd gained a foothold outside traditional VNA services, and our staff count was just over one hundred.

In July 1984, three days after I assumed my new role as executive director, the CEO of the medical center—I'll call him T.—called our office. Our agency had never received a call from him before. The medical center operated its own small VNA—one of the eight—but the CEO was usually focused on more pressing hospital revenue drivers, so I was surprised by his call. To be honest, I was flattered.

Congenial and direct, two traits I admire in businesspeople, the CEO inquired about my plans as the agency's new head and offered his ear if I needed one. He and I knew each other by reputation, as I was on the board of community organizations, including a smaller hospital, where members of his executive team served alongside me.

"What would you think of a potential merger of home health agencies?"

There was a pause I didn't know how to fill.

"We'd all benefit from greater efficiency, and we could create scale," he went on.

Intellectually, I wasn't opposed. I liked change. If his question seemed brazen for a first conversation, I assumed he was trustworthy.

"There's incentive for us," he offered. "Our visiting nurse service is small, and we need a capable agency to discharge our patients to." He had the referrals, he was saying, while we had the skill and the scale.

We aligned over the inherent inefficiency of a major medical center discharging patients to eight different agencies. At the end of our first conversation, he pointed out that we had each come to our roles differently than most CEOs of medical centers and VNAs—he wasn't a doctor, and I wasn't a nurse. Later, I'd wonder if that was part of how he seduced me; twenty years my senior, he was inviting me into his club.

Over the next six months, we spent hours on the phone, thinking broadly about how we might bring the agencies together. He'd call with a potential problem he saw; I'd respond with a solution. I liked having a smart executive to talk to. I saw us as collaborators. Still, from early on, I made it clear I would not engage my board in this merger without job protection, and that my interest was in being CEO of any new entity. He said he understood.

A few months into our work, we had put together a business plan. He asked me to present our three-year financial pro formas to a group of executives as a trial run.

Two things stand out from that meeting: I was the only woman in a room of six dark-suited men, all from the upper echelon of the medical center, and they didn't look like they knew what to do with me—as if they didn't quite believe a woman could have constructed this plan. They smiled politely but hesitated to dig in. In that time, at that level, this was a men's table, especially where money was counted and strategic decisions were made.

"No need to stand," I said, shaking the hands of each of the VPs, before taking my place at the conference table.

I covered the business plan and waited for reactions. There were none at first. I was used to my team and board firing questions, pushing on assumptions, advocating for programs.

Finally, a consulting CPA, brought in by T., spoke up. "Have you ever thought about going into consulting?" he asked, smiling.

The question struck me as odd at the time, but I tucked it away for later.

"Obviously," he added, looking around at the other men, "you've knocked our socks off."

Dozens of meetings followed as we dug into the details, engaging the eight executive directors and their boards in the benefits and challenges of making this new agency happen. As the months wore on, I noticed more and more men from T.'s gang at our meetings, as if eight agencies that had run successfully for fifty years without them couldn't handle something bigger.

When it came time for the interim board to select its new CEO, T. informed me there'd be a national search. I balked, but he said this was routine procedure for the medical center and his VNA board would insist upon it. I was green. I'd thought he had my back—and that he would have managed the internal bureaucracy and politics of his center.

"That's not what you implied," I said.

"You'll apply," he said. "It will work out fine."

But it didn't work out fine.

The interim board split fifty-fifty between me and a Boston friend of T.'s. I was learning that no matter how well our community agencies were run, it was the medical center that wielded the power. They had the patients to discharge. They were the larger organization.

Stymied, the interim board took what I would later call the lazy route: they said they could hire both of us, one as CEO and one as COO, as long as we could agree on who would be which.

This was preposterous. Neither of us had applied to be #2. But I was in too deep and still believed that T. would support me in the end.

The other candidate and I sat across from each other that afternoon, and I quickly learned she was twenty years my senior, was nearing retirement, saw this as her final job, had only worked in urban medical settings, and was a nurse. The board's split seemed to be between MSN vs. MBA, older vs. younger, hospital- vs. community-based.

"So, do you want to be COO?" I asked.

"Of course not."

"Neither do I."

There was little more to say.

When I called T. at home to give him our news, I said, "Sorry. Neither of us is interested in being second. I'm handing this problem back to you."

OUT ON THE FAIRWAY, I SEE FOUR MEN advancing. Three more are practicing putts on the putting green. The meadowlark continues to hop from branch to branch, spitting chaff from its beak. The wildness of this bird grabs me, and I think about how mundane our human worries are much of the time. Back in 1984, I was still under the influence of outdated myths about men—which often led me to hand over my own authority to them. Staring at the bird, I see that I did with T. what I had done with my father. With both, I'd believed they were trustworthy; I'd relaxed my boundaries around them, and I'd ceded my power.

The merger failed. My board pulled out, citing discontent with the medical center's political maneuvering by putting their nurse friend in contention for CEO.

The following year, while getting our agency back on its feet, the executive director of the VNA across the Connecticut River in Vermont asked if we might merge on our own. She was nearing retirement and liked the way our board and executive team made decisions. We brought the two agencies together easily and in six months became the first bi-state VNA in the country. Over the next decade, the other six agencies would come under a joint umbrella and eventually become the large agency that now serves all of New Hampshire and Vermont.

I stayed on for a year to integrate the Vermont merger, but I knew it was time to leave, to see what I could make of myself in the larger world of business, outside of our parochial region. I picked up the CPA's consulting question and, after considering joining his firm in the health-care division, decided to form my own company. Even as a young advisor to CEOs, I knew there had to be better ways to help companies grow and change that wouldn't traumatize the people involved.

We learn about trust in our families—and if those lessons aren't good ones, we have to learn as adults. We also learn from our failures. The failed merger had taught me everything I needed to know about how often I still believed the hype about powerful men when frequently they disappointed me. Even if patriarchy ruled back then—and still does—it was easy to see that men weren't inherently superior. They had no corner on intellect or decision-making. They were often shortsighted, non-intuitive, and clung to outmoded communication forms. But I still didn't know how to claim *my* power in partnership with them. As I changed, they too changed how they worked with me. The best of them could see that together we had the potential to transform the cultures of their companies. It was a potent time, when women were beginning to be brought into corner suites and onto boards, a time when the best CEOs saw the value of our gender difference and a non-male brand of leadership at the table. I served as a proxy during that transitional time and would see that proxy repeated later as the first people of color and LGBTQ leaders entered the highest positions in the corporate world.

Sitting by the golf course in Austin, I see that I had hoped powerful men in my adulthood would be different from my father. Businessmen talked differently, acted differently, cared about different things, and some of them were authentically different, but what attracted me—whether to my father and the literary men around him, George Hormel and my grandfather, or the men I was advising—was their innate *expectation* to get what they wanted, a learned assumption I'd not been born into. As I changed my orientation to male power, more CEOs hired me, and my business took off.

I wonder if my grandfather's faith in George Hormel was too strong. I wonder if, after twenty years, he'd trusted him to have his back after the embezzlement. That wouldn't happen. And I wonder if my father's telling of the embezzlement as a mythology of good versus evil acted like a smoke screen preventing me from seeing what I could have seen earlier—that the luster of A.L.'s twenty-year partnership with George was likely fragmenting, at the same time as the embezzlement was underway.

Two years ago, when I was here with El, I never imagined these questions. I've been trying to corral A.L. and George Hormel—big and unwieldy and impossible to entirely know—into a finite pen like I might two hogs. But they keep dodging and weaving. And my perception of them keeps changing.

Sitting under the shade of this maple tree, still keeping an eye out for Michael, I think that discovering whatever George and A.L. did or didn't do, knew or didn't know, will no longer devastate me, nor redeem me. I'll just know what happened. And knowing will enable me to move on.

10.

A Cyclone Lands

Austin

1906–1910

My father used to tell me that when he was a little boy, the best part of his day was when his father returned from the meat factory, or from selling on the road. Dad and Dryden would lean out from the wide veranda at 811 Kenwood Avenue, watching for A.L.'s black car to pull up the short drive—or, if it was winter, the two boys would paste their noses to the parlor window. When they spotted the car—an early Model T by Henry Ford—the boys would leap off the porch, scamper down the path, and jump into A.L.'s arms, each racing to be first.

This ritual guaranteed two things: first, each day, one of the boys would miss the mark, fall to the ground, scrape his knee, and call to his mother for rescue; and second, a competitive spirit was born early in the Eberhart boys.

Where A.L. encouraged athletics and outdoor activities, Lena trained her children in the arts, music, and literature, raising my father on Shakespeare and Wordsworth. A.L. played catch with his children, read them popular books, and took them on camping trips. A card-carrying member of the National Rifle Association, he loved to hunt and fish, and as a member of the Republican Party, he closely followed the politics and news of the time. If he was an old-school Republican, my father said Lena was more new-day Democrat, especially concerned about the conditions of those less fortunate.

As the light faded each evening, Lena and A.L. gathered their sons to the piano, where A.L. played and she sang. The boys squeezed up to either side of their father as Lena stood beside. If winter snowstorms kept the family indoors, they pulled out backgammon and bridge.

Each summer, Chautauqua arrived in Austin, and Lena made sure her children were present. The Chautauqua movement had spread across the Northeast and Midwest after the Civil War, as oratory and elocution skills were increasingly admired. My father heard speeches on religion, temperance, and the labor movement. Politicians toured the Chautauqua circuit, as it filled a role that radio and TV would later step into. In dinner conversations, Lena and A.L. made use of Chautauqua to engage their children in the affairs of the time. The family immersed itself in the cultural opportunities afforded them and were keen observers of it all.

What struck me in reading my grandfather's letters and my father's journals of that time was how involved Lena was in her husband's business life and how engaged A.L. was in his children's upbringing. Their marriage was a partnership between equally smart and invested adults that blurred early lines of gender roles and expectations.

IN 1908, THE HORMEL COMPANY BUILT a new administrative office next to its packing plant. In the seven years that A.L. had been in Austin, the company's net sales had grown to over $3 million (about $93 million today), and its net earnings to over $1 million (about $31 million today). My grandfather rarely got salary increases, but it was made up for in being paid 10 percent of that million, as agreed on hiring, and by his additional certificates of stock. He was doing well. In a population of 6,000, only eight citizens of Austin owned cars that year, of which two belonged to A.L.

That summer was a good one. As the stores of ice blocks melted in the Hormel icehouse and there was no way to protect raw meat, the factory closed down, as it did every year when ice ran out. A.L. took his family and three colleagues and their wives to the boundary waters of northern Minnesota. They traveled in auto caravans filled with camping gear, fishing poles, and rifles and stayed at a fishing lodge. In the north they swam, fished, and shot ducks for dinner. Each photograph from that trip is inscribed in A.L.'s hand. "Roughing it," reads one in which Lena is lying in a hammock in the shade.

TWO YEARS EARLIER, ON JUNE 18, 1906, a twenty-year-old named Ransome J. Thomson had arrived at George Hormel's office asking for a job. George had an abrupt countenance and impatience with young people. He wasn't going to waste any words that day.

"So, you're Alec Thomson's boy?" he asked.

Alec Thomson had been doing contract business with George as a livestock dealer in LeRoy, Minnesota. After his sons had completed high school, he and his wife traded in their meager family farm so Alec could be employed directly by Geo. A. Hormel & Company as an animal dealer. Cy's mother had written letters to her son describing the fine Hormel enterprise Alec was working for, and suggesting it might need a young man like him. Cy and his new wife Maude took a gamble, moved in with Cy's parents, and Cy went to seek work there.

"So, you want a job?" George asked.

"Yes, sir," Cy said.

"Well, I guess we can use another young fellow. Willing to start at twelve dollars a week?"

"Yes, sir."

George, who liked putting to work the younger relatives of tried and true employees, sized up the slightly built young man in front of him— thin black hair, eyes positioned narrowly on his face—and thought he didn't look like one for prodding hogs toward the kill chute, nor for heaving carcasses to the killing floor. He did, however, look just right for an inside job.

R. J. THOMSON

"Come to work on Monday," he told Cy. "Report to Fred Ulme in the fresh department as a scaler."

Cy would later write that his first job required *fidelity, alertness, and a mind ready with figures*. His tasks replicated those of a shipping clerk, checking weights and contents of meat parcels as they left the packing floor for the shipping room and reporting each figure to his superior at the end of the day.

The Hormel company was the biggest, maybe best, employer for miles around, and paid better wages than most while giving employees (albeit unpaid) time off each summer. Cy would later say he'd landed where he wanted to be.

RANSOME JOSIAH THOMSON WAS BORN on January 27, 1886, in the small, rural town of Cresco, Iowa, just over the southern Minnesota border, where his father first held a position as grain buyer for a local company. Cy's childhood was spent alongside seven siblings in a simple pioneer house built by his grandparents.

Growing up in the era of whooping cough and measles, Ransome and his brothers and sisters were invariably sick, and their parents were strapped to care for the rambunctious brood—especially their eighth child, who quickly earned the nickname "Cyclone" for his agitated, constant movement. Later, his nickname was shortened to "Cy."

Cy claimed he was an introverted and sensitive child who lacked a confidant, despite his many siblings. Even growing up, he said, he'd craved the attention and acclaim of others, and he would later cite that need as one reason for his criminal activity. But he quickly showed a natural aptitude for numbers.

As a young boy, a family friend gave Cy three crisp dollar bills and encouraged him to invest them in something worthy that would return him a profit. More important to Cy than the money itself was the confidence his benefactor had in his business acumen. His father encouraged him to invest in pigs or sheep. The following day, Cy took the family carriage horse and buggy on a ten-mile road trip to bargain for pigs. For his three dollar bills, he got six of them. He raised his pigs and by the end of the summer had made enough money to buy a dozen sheep, along with the fencing needed to keep them penned. He continued trading in sheep until high school and dreamed of one day raising the most perfect animal bloodlines, be they sheep, hogs, cattle, or chickens.

Cy's early years were spent ten miles down the road from W.I. Wells, head of the notorious Wells gang. Wells and Alec Thomson knew each other, and Cy claims he grew up on stories of the Wells gang, along with their friends Jesse James and the Younger brothers, who planned to rob a bank in Northfield, Minnesota. On their way to Northfield, James and the Youngers spent several days in LeRoy visiting the Wells's headquarters, and some of the Wells brothers served as guides for Jesse James as he set off to rob the bank. In the aftermath of the attempted robbery, two of the Wells brothers were shot and killed. Cy would later claim that his parents romanticized these crimes and would blame them, in part, for his wrongdoings.

While in high school, Cy fell in love with a young woman three years older and from *a better clan*. Maude Goss was a senior and, after graduating, she picked up a teaching job in South Dakota, where an uncle lived. Three years later, Cy followed her to teach in a nearby school district, but his initial interest in teaching waned over that year, while their relationship continued to blossom. Growing up, the only model for adult work that Cy had known was the hard day-labor of his father and grandfather. He assumed this would be his lot in life too.

THROUGH HIS FIRST MONTHS AS A HORMEL company scaler, Cy kept his head down and performed his work well. But by the spring of 1907, he itched for more.

It was around this time that he bought himself one share of Hormel stock. Maybe he wanted a piece of the company his father was working for. Maybe he was promising himself a better life than his parents and grandparents had made for themselves. Either way, he sized up the Hormel company as growing fast and needing young men like him.

Frustrated with his low wage and responsibility, Cy sought his second meeting with George Hormel. Stern and often silent, George's countenance discouraged conversation. Cy wanted an administrative job, one where he'd be a central part of the company's action. He prepared a full speech for his boss, while believing George's positive relationship with his father, Alec, augured for a positive response. George had long preferred developing the talent of local boys. He would later write, *I wanted the country boys who came to work for us to be so good and efficient that when an opportunity arose [inside the company], they, and not outside talent, would fill the better job. Bright boys in our town would have no reason to go off to big cities when economic success was possible right at home.*

"You're right, young man, you could have a better job," George told Cy. "But to make more money and have more responsibility, you'll need more education. And currently, we have no openings in our administrative offices."

According to Cy, he proposed on the spot to attend Mankato Commercial College, sixty miles northwest of Austin, to procure degrees in bookkeeping and stenography, and George promised him a job upon completion. Cy pulled together his meager savings from teaching school, bade Maude goodbye for three months, and ventured north for the summer. Conversely, George Hormel alleges in *The Open Road* that he offered to subsidize Cy's education, as he liked the young man's industry and saw in him an earlier version of his once-scrappy self.

Whether Cy or George financed the Mankato education, at the end of the summer Cy returned to Austin, presented his two diplomas, and watched George nearly gush at the first person in his employ with professional business training.

"I believe we want young fellows with that much initiative in our concern," he said, and gave Cy a job as a clerk and stenographer in the company's central office.

Now no longer among factory workers inside jumbled buildings, Cy sat in proximity to company administrative staff and executives. He witnessed the circulation of correspondence and business documents. He listened to men making decisions.

He saw that life was better upstairs, where men dressed in tailored suits, women wore long skirts and button-up blouses, and the executives went home for their noonday meals. Even the air was fresher upstairs, free of the putrid smell that coursed through the packinghouse.

Small promotions came quickly, and each improvement garnered a small increase in pay. In 1908, Cy was named company cashier and given a salary of thirty-five dollars a week. At twenty-one, he was entrusted with hundreds of thousands of company dollars and reported to A.L. Eberhart. By this time, he was dressing in suits like his bosses, transitioning as easily from his scaler's smock as George Hormel had from his butcher's apron. Cy had a keen eye for class distinctions, later writing that *a good front is everything for a man. Business associates take you at your clothes' value.*

An inventive and quick learner, Cy set about to reorganize several administrative departments, improving their productivity and efficiency. At the age of twenty-five, he was rewarded with the title of assistant comptroller and was supervised by the company's comptroller, E.S. Selby. This job made him responsible for the company's general ledger, categorizing and accumulating all financial accounts into one place for accurate reference. He maintained a list of the company's fixed assets and reported regularly on its cash. And he was now responsible for the transfer of funds between the company's bank accounts.

Until 1994, when the Riegle-Neal Interstate Banking and Branching Efficiency Act was made into law, there were few places where banks were allowed to do business outside their home states. In 1900, a good-sized company like Geo. A. Hormel & Company would have had dozens of bank accounts in numerous banks across multiple states. These banking relationships grew as its network of sales offices grew. Banks were needed for working capital and operating loans, accepting and securing deposits, and managing company wire transfers. Nearly everything—including recording sales and revenue in the accounting system before sending on cash by courier or mail to the appropriate bank—was done by hand. Several days or a week might go by before funds were fully processed and posted to the proper account.

CY WORKED LONG HOURS AND ESCHEWED time off. If he saw a need in the community of Austin, he pitched in to help. Over time, he became known as, and loved for being, a significant benefactor. If an organizing committee was planning a town event but couldn't afford a covered wagon for its display, he would step in and buy the wagon. If the wagon was in a different state, he'd fund its transportation to Austin. If Cy encountered a down-on-his-luck person on the street, he provided cash to give him a better day. It's no wonder that he was later referred to as a *generous embezzler*.

Cy and Maude joined the Congregational Church in Austin, which he referred to as the town's *society church*—the one where the elites, like the Eberharts and Catherwoods, congregated. Cy taught Sunday school and eventually became the school's superintendent. He gained valuable contact with influential people, including Hormel executives, leading them to trust him and procuring for him even greater responsibility in the company. Later, he'd say he was satisfying a craving to stand shoulder to shoulder with men in power.

From his prison cell, he'd write, *It all dovetailed together very nicely*.

11.

Rock Star Status in a Small Midwestern City

Austin

2000

"Here we go," I say to my brother, Dikkon, as we disembark our plane in Minneapolis.

He raises his eyebrows in agreement.

We've flown in from Boston to represent our father at a citywide, three-day celebration to rename Austin's high school library after him. I've brought a laptop full of notes from my prior two visits to Austin, along with a videotaped message from Dad about his childhood in Minnesota that we'll show at the assembly.

We're both excited to be here, though maybe for different reasons. Dikkon—fifty-four years old, while I'm forty-nine—loves this kind of celebration, where he can play up the role of "son of a literary figure" and tell his best famous-writer stories. I'm more ambivalent. As my father has aged and since my mother died, I've been increasingly called on to play the role of his surrogate while concurrently reckoning with his molestation of me. The prospect of three days lauding my father makes me feel like an imposter. But I want to see Ella Marie and Knowles again, and to continue learning about what happened to my grandfather. That eagerness supersedes what this weekend will require of me.

My father is ninety-six now. Back in August, I visited him in his retirement home in New Hampshire. I helped him sort through his mail while I was there, and in the pile was an invitation from the Austin High School Alumni & Friends Association laying out its annual event, this year celebrating him. I talked it up and asked Dad if he'd like to accept.

"I can't go," he said, his eyes searching the floor.

"Are you sure?"

Dad is still scratching out poems on the backs of envelopes, but his world is smaller now. In that moment, without Mom there to encourage him, he looked unable to muster what it would take.

"They're expecting a lot, Dad," I said, rereading the list of activities the committee had planned. "It's okay not to go if you don't want to."

"You go," he said, surprising me.

"Really?" I asked.

As we talked it through, I wondered aloud if Dikkon might like to go with me.

"That would be marvelous," Dad said, a smile returning to his face.

OUTSIDE THE AIRPORT, WE'RE SURPRISED by a white stretch limousine and a group of friendly people with "Eberhart" signs. My stomach turns, fearing I won't be able to meet the group's expectations. I think of calls I've had from editors of the *New York Times* and the *Los Angeles Review of Books*, seeking comments about the deaths of my father's poet friends. I can assist my father in those situations because I know how he feels about his friends, but here I feel uneasy as his ambassador. Staring at the limo as the greeting committee converses around me, my mind toggles between disappointment in my father and pride in his literary achievements. I feel guilty for accepting this invitation, but here I am.

I climb inside the stretch limo and lean back against its plush white leather. Champagne is poured into slender glass flutes and passed around. It's 2:00 p.m. on a sunny afternoon. The champagne loosens me. Maybe I can let this be okay, as it reminds me of the fun parts of growing up in proximity to a star.

I smile at Dikkon across our rolling living room and tip my glass, as if to say, *I could get used to this—you?*

Out the windows, I take in the vast Minnesota grain fields, turned over for winter, as black as French roast coffee grounds. A blue sky hangs above us. How can I possibly hold all that happened here while still not knowing all that truly did, and simultaneously celebrate my father?

Jeni Lindberg, the event's organizer—she's about four years younger than I am—is joined by two journalists: Bob Vilt, reporter for the *Austin Herald* and one of Jeni's high school classmates, and a reporter for the *Minneapolis Star Tribune* whose name I've missed.

"We understand you knew Frost?" Bob asks.

Dikkon nods, happy to take this one. "We moved to Hanover in 1956 when Dad succeeded Frost as poet-in-residence at Dartmouth. Robert was at our house frequently. That was lucky for me when I was in fifth grade."

The reporters hunch forward, scratching notes on their pads.

"My teacher assigned a Frost poem for homework, I can't remember which," Dikkon continues, "and we were told to come back to class the next morning with our interpretation of what was meant by its last line." A grin spreads across my brother's face. He's enjoying this. "*That's easy,* I thought. *I'll ask Mr. Frost over dinner.*"

He's giving the reporters what they want—a few nuggets for their newspapers and a little reflection of how we grew up. I know our childhood impresses people, but it's unearned attention. It didn't have anything to do with me or Dikkon.

"What about Allen Ginsberg?" the *Star Tribune* reporter asks. "We know your father had a strong connection with him."

I take this one. Allen was one of the few of Dad's friends who treated me like an adult in my teens, not just as a kid hanging around the poets.

"I met him when I was seventeen," I say, emboldened by the champagne. "He was a practicing Buddhist by then, and he and his partner, Peter Orlovsky, were staying with us. I'd just come back from a year of boarding school in Lausanne. They'd just been in India. We talked about Buddhism and the war in Vietnam and our views on this country when we were looking at it from overseas. What I remember is how down-to-earth they both were."

"Wonderful," Bob says from my periphery. "I'll lead with that for the *Herald.*"

"Does your father ever talk about Austin?" Jeni asks.

"Frequently," I say, which is true. "He describes his childhood here as idyllic. He wrote his first poems here. He quarterbacked the football team."

Prior to this trip, I emailed Jeni about my grandfather's mixed experience in Austin—helping build the Hormel company, being fired by George Hormel—so there's context for me to be frank.

"But he anguished over his father's firing," I continue, "and to this day he grieves his mother's painful death to cancer. His family grew and prospered here—it was their 'American dream.' But they lost the dream here too. My father's never gotten over that."

There's a quiet space I feel no need to fill. Dikkon raises his eyebrows at me, and I suspect he'd prefer me not to open that family lid further. The reporters jot their notes.

"Well, here's what we have planned for you," Jeni says, handing Dikkon and me copies of an itinerary covering the next three days.

I scan the pages and see that every hour is filled with media interviews, presentations before large crowds, and visits to elementary school classrooms. We're riding in the lead convertible during a citywide parade. We'll be introduced under lights in front of thousands at the Friday night football game. We're expected to speak on behalf of our father at the all-school-district assembly and to attend the renaming ceremony. We'll also attend a poetry slam scheduled at the public library.

My stomach is in knots. I hadn't factored in how emotional it might be to spend three days celebrating the very myths about my father that I'm trying to dismantle.

I glance out the window and watch wispy clouds waltz over the plains. The group breaks into laughter. Their faces are full of anticipation; they've worked hard to pull this off. I'm touched. What other small midwestern city would charge all five thousand of its schoolchildren, kindergarten through twelfth grade, with studying the work of one poet and then trying their hand at the craft?

The limo rolls into town and pulls into the new Holiday Inn. Our driver reaches for my hand and helps me out onto the shiny black tarmac. He points to the brand-new gold-painted van, keys in the ignition, free for our use through the weekend. Jeni's committee has thought of everything. We wave to our hosts and turn to check in at the front desk.

On the registration counter are two copies of today's *Austin Herald*. The paper includes a full-page story announcing our arrival. Dikkon picks up his copy, smiles, and hands me mine.

12.

Let the Good Times Roll

Austin

1905–1915

In 1905, Geo. A. Hormel & Company sailed through its fifth anniversary, headed toward a full decade of prosperity. George's promise to his mother that rather than end up a hog butcher he would become a meatpacker had materialized. Now, he was someone who hired men below him to do the bloody business of killing and cutting up pigs, and focused his own talent on organizing people and creating standards for his operations. In giving up his cleaver, donning woolen suits, and becoming a company president, he'd achieved a position never known in his family.

He kept a daily routine, taking early breakfast with his wife, Lillian; riding his horse one mile to the factory—until he purchased his first car—and spending his mornings on administrative chores. After returning home for his midday meal, he went back to the factory and walked its floors, ensuring every cleaver and knife was sharpened to a razor's edge. He reacted quickly to problems, didn't think deeply about them, kept greasing his cogs of production. Later, he would think about what it meant to be an early industrialist

in the dawning of the twentieth century, but the present was awash in operational details, and that's where he focused. If occasionally he praised a cutter for proper trimming of fat from a ham, he spent more time criticizing one man's work before moving to the next.

"No trimmings on the floor," he'd say firmly to a cutter contorted over his table.

"Clean up this room," he'd bark to another, pinching his eyes and pursing his lips.

In his defense, he'd later write, *my insistence on perfection was not a joke. I was incessantly preaching that we were engaged in one of the most important tasks in the world—feeding people.*

His mother's lesson that a job done right the first time saved time, paired with his uncle Decker's admonishment that clean meat makes you money, had made him a fanatic not only for perfection, but for cleanliness. He'd seen enough filth in his early life and in the Chicago meatpacking houses to want no more of it.

While constantly on the search for men to work in the packing house, George introduced an on-site laundry in 1903.

This was a benefit to the butchers, as their aprons would be cleaned at company expense and they would no longer need to take their soiled aprons home with them, but it was also good for the company, as blood pathogens would be cleaned out of the fabric every day. Federal inspectors liked a clean packinghouse, and noted George's intention to create the cleanest in the industry. That same year, the company hired a Kansas City architect to remodel and enlarge the Austin packing plant, adding a three-story hog-kill building, a two-story beef-kill space, an engine room and machine shop, and a sausage casing department. In 1905, it added a five-story curing building.

In 1908, the company rebuilt its administrative and executive headquarters. Until then nearly everyone with an administrative function—salesmen, clerks, stenographers, executives—had worked near each other, their desks jammed together across an open room. George Hormel sat at his desk against the back wall. A.L. sat in the middle of the room, stealing light from the window to his left. My father would describe how noisy the headquarters were—"a hive of activity," he'd say—with creaking floorboards, tapping stenographers, and whistling wind leaking through the windows.

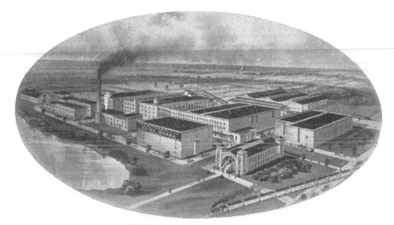

GEORGE A. HORMEL & CO.

The new space, on the lower right side of the campus, gave executives their own offices, with privacy for meetings and dictating correspondence. Described as "elegant" in the company's seventy-five anniversary book, the renovations included paneled oak on the walls and Italian terrazzo laid on the floors. Company workers assisted in its construction by making lime and cement bricks for the outside facade, while a large bronze door was hung to mark the new corporate entrance. A dedicated boardroom was created for director meetings and conferencing. Before this, board meetings had been informal affairs, held in the Hormels' front parlor or in the Eberharts' sitting room. Following a board meeting, Lena or Lillian would provide the men with a four-course meal. Now, the directors would meet at company headquarters.

That same year, a business partnership ended, bringing all company assets under the name of Geo. A. Hormel & Company. This change meant the loss of three members of the board. Lena Eberhart and Lillian Hormel were recruited to fill two of their seats. They would remain directors through the next six years, until 1914.

Lena and Lillian both originated, tasted, and tested recipes for new Hormel products. My father used to say that Lena knew the intentions of A.L.'s business trips, knew personally many of his professional relationships, and, while the conversations weren't carried on in front of the children, he could see that Lena was A.L.'s confidante.

It was unusual for women to serve on corporate boards back then—only somewhat less so today—but Lillian and Lena were smart, independent thinkers, and highly respected women in Austin. If you didn't count gender, they'd have been natural picks, and they were insiders, which made them trustworthy. With both of them on the company board, A.L. and Lena must have felt like they were almost part of the Hormel family.

LIKE GEORGE, A.L HAD HIS ROUTINES, BUT HE was prone to prioritize his people. He'd long done away with the selling systems he'd inherited from his boss, where three Hormel brothers were dispatched as road salesmen on horseback and bicycles. That strategy would never create a national brand. As A.L. opened the next fourteen Hormel sales branches, he and George were driven, as most company leaders are, to grow the enterprise; if they didn't, they knew the company would become irrelevant and might fail. A.L. cultivated relationships across the country and kept in touch with each of them by way of a vigorous correspondence.

In 1910, Lena and A.L. welcomed their third child, Elizabeth Ann, an immediate pleasure to them. While Richard and Dryden enjoyed athletics, Elizabeth followed her mother through the gardens and kitchen. She observed her parents' and siblings' interactions, honing her instincts for understanding family dynamics. It's not surprising that in young adulthood she chose a college degree in social work and went on to have

a long career in the field, well into her late seventies. Aunt Bunny, as I called her, told me she'd felt deeply loved by both her parents.

In 1911, the Hormel company killed 32,646 hogs, a near 40 percent increase from the year before. A photograph of the key staff at Geo. A. Hormel & Company on the front steps of the new executive building shows Cy Thomson and A.L. Eberhart directly in front of the door. As Richard Dougherty wrote in the company's seventy-fifth anniversary book about that year, George Hormel thought *the road ahead looked clear and bright.* Along with the company's expansion and prosperity, the wealth of both the Hormels and the Eberharts grew.

THROUGH THIS DECADE, A.L. TOOK HIS FAMILY on yearly trips through New Mexico, Arizona, and Colorado. In Tennessee and Louisiana, he and Lena toured sharecropper farms and conversed with Black farmers about how they produced and moved cotton, a topic useful to him with his cotton broker friends in Texas. He enjoyed connecting with people, listening to their stories and evolving his understanding of the world with them.

In 1919, two years before the embezzlement was discovered, my grandparents took their longest trip, leaving their children (then seventeen, fifteen, and eight) at home with friends. In automobiles and on trains, they toured South Dakota, Wyoming, Utah, and Nevada, all the way to San Francisco. While staying there, they boarded a train up Mount Tamalpais, and continued their tour south to Los Angeles, where they traveled down Rodeo Drive, then just a wide clay street edged by palm trees. Photos from the Grand Canyon show Lena with friends on horses, smiling into the camera before descending to the Colorado River.

When they weren't traveling outside of Austin, the Eberharts, Hormels, and other prominent families spent part of their summers along the Red Cedar River in large canvas tents on platforms. They fitted their tents with iceboxes, telephones, and electric lights. Families brought their pianos and organs, their rowboats and canoes, their fishing poles and cigars. They brought their hired help. A milkman and dairyman came every day to deliver fresh milk, eggs, and butter. The Eberhart and Hormel camps, apparently located next to each other, were named "Riverside." Lena's best friend Adah Crane and her husband Ralph's camp was named "Crane's Nest." I assume the Catherwood family summered there too, though I never got a chance to ask Betty.

Those summer days of swimming, fishing for bass, and paddling canoes up to Ramsey wove through my father's stories. He and Dryden learned every turn of the winding river while his parents kept to the shade of a burr oak on its bank. Each evening, crackling fires lit up the sky.

Meanwhile, with the company in peak expansion, my grandfather probably felt as if he'd hooked himself to a booster rocket of sales, one he just needed to keep aloft. I have no doubt that during those summers, my grandfather had full faith in himself and his partners in the packing plant. He likely looked forward to many more years at Geo. A. Hormel & Company.

WITH A FISCAL CALENDAR STARTING ON OCTOBER 1, the Hormel company borrowed heavily each year for working capital to buy hogs, finance factory expansions, and pay wages, just as its agrarian predecessors had done for decades.

Cy Thomson, former farm boy, now charged with tracking financial details for the company, knew this agrarian calendar, and the intricate financial needs of the company, but he still yearned to be higher up, in the top echelon of Austin businessmen.

Luck fell his way. Cy's supervisor, the company's comptroller, E.S. Selby, left his job abruptly, and Cy was the only one in the accounting department familiar with making bank transactions and who had a working knowledge of foreign exchange. He was immediately promoted without a new title, taking over the full task and responsibility of his former boss, and essentially stepping into the role of the company comptroller—some sources name him that. I've wondered if this was one of George Hormel's impulsive moves. But why wouldn't he have promoted Cy? He trusted him, and with the company growing exponentially, there was little time to look for someone else.

EARLY IN 1911, WHILE A.L. WAS CREATING A NEW sales team and distribution center in San Antonio, Cy Thomson made his first steal—one he later claimed to have done without pre-planning or immediate use for the money.

A Mrs. Mary Hollingshead from South Dakota had mailed the company $800 in cash (about $24,000 today) for the purchase of eight shares of stock. Cy mailed her the certificates while *letting the currency burn a hole in [his] pocket*, as he'd later write. He fashioned a false accounting record to identify both the income and expense in the company's official books, then immediately felt conflicted. He'd just gained $800, which amounted to a 40 percent increase in his $2,000 annual wage, but if he spent it, he'd likely call attention to himself, to his banker, maybe to his wife. He had to conjure a way to make this new cash look okay.

Cy solved this problem by selling the first share of Hormel stock he'd bought years earlier for a tidy profit and letting everyone around him know that he'd done so. This gave him cover for using the $800 he'd stolen. As he later wrote about the incident from his cell, he appeared not to understand his own motivation. *If ever a theft was committed from sheer impulse*, he wrote, *this was one. I have laid awake many nights, trying to figure out why I first became a thief. But in all sincerity, I cannot yet truly tell why I took my first step into the quicksand.*

With that as his start, Cy continued stealing while also starting to invest in the stock market and in real estate, buying himself additional cover. He talked up every windfall and each loss, giving the impression that anything tangible he owned had been rightfully gained. He also started spreading the lie that he'd inherited money, and, in some records, some of his land, from a wealthy aunt and had invested his money well. Along with everyone else, George and A.L. believed him.

Months after his first theft, Cy purchased his first car. Now he could move around southern Minnesota with greater speed. One evening, he took Maude for a scenic drive south of Austin to their hometown of LeRoy. The Thomson farmstead had been sold when Cy's father took his full-time position at Geo. A. Hormel & Company. The single, older woman who'd bought the place was now having a hard time maintaining it on her own.

"I'd like to sell it," she confided to Cy. "I just can't keep it up."

Cy's brain churned as he took in this opportunity. As quick to decisions as the weather event he'd been named for, he reasoned he could buy back his family homestead while helping out this poor woman.

"I'll take it for $1,300," he said, "and I'll bring the money tomorrow."

Now he was committed. He'd bought a car with the first $800 he'd stolen. To purchase the homestead, he'd have to steal more cash.

ONCE THE TRANSACTION WAS SEALED AND THE old farmhouse in LeRoy was Cy's, people asked what he intended to do with it.

"Raise chickens," he said.

In time, he did just that, creating what was reputed to be the largest poultry farm in the country—some said the world—with more than 20,000 Leghorns and a rooster valued at $10,000. Cy gutted and rebuilt barns, ordered his first thousand White Leghorn chicks, and went into business. The more he built, the more he had to steal; or the more he stole, the more he could build. Who knew which came first?

He hired a farm manager to oversee his poultry and installed the best air-circulating system to ensure the health of his birds. According to legend, one year Cy's birds took home more prizes at poultry shows than any on three continents. Next to the Hormel company, Oak Dale Farms, as he eventually would call his enterprise, must have been one of the largest businesses in southern Minnesota.

As his building campaign escalated, Cy became hypervigilant. Unlike the one share of Hormel stock he'd purchased and sold (or could have held on to and watched grow patiently for years) his life became a nonstop obstacle course as he took more and more money from the company, invested more and more in Oak Dale Farms, and had to figure out novel ways to cover his tracks.

Hypervigilance is an extreme form of anxiety and takes a psychological toll. Worry over being found out, worry over maintaining books that would look accurate to executives and auditors, worry about keeping his reputation polished both inside and outside the company—it all put Cy in a constant state of agitation, which, since he'd been young, was his natural state of being. But in George Hormel's fast-growing company, most minds were on plant renovations, new sales offices, a constant stream of hiring, and expanding production. This worked to Cy's advantage. George was a member of the Austin selectboard. A.L. was a member of the chamber of commerce. The executives were up to their eyeballs in community commitments. As long as the books were balanced, no one had reason to suspect that Cy was doing anything but an exceptional job. While the company seemed to be consuming great sums of cash, that didn't strike anyone as terribly unusual given its fast track.

Cy was in too deep to stop. George had long ago given up his twin vices of gambling and tobacco chewing before they could become real problems, habits he'd known were doing him no good and marked him as a butcher, not a meatpacker. In contrast, Cy was fully addicted to stealing and couldn't stop. And his addiction was criminal. Staying alert to the mail coming in and going out, to the people around him, and continually covering his tracks, consumed his life. While maintaining hundreds of transactions, he schemed constantly.

BY 1914, THE HORMEL COMPANY WAS EMPLOYING more than three hundred people, though it was persistently needing more, and George had given up trying to oversee every decision and transaction beneath him. At various times, Cy's supervision seems to have fallen to several men, including at the end, George's son, Jay.

Jay Catherwood Hormel, born on September 11, 1892, and a graduate of Austin High School in 1912, wanted to attend military college but went to Princeton upon his father's insistence. He was the first member of the Hormel family to attend university, but he professed more interest in factory work than college and dropped out of Princeton after only two years to return to Austin to work in the family company.

George would later claim that on more than one occasion, he asked Cy directly about his spending, and Cy demurred. Bankers and auditors never called attention to any accounting problems. Cy brought to the office not only an uncanny work ethic but also a sunny outlook. He had a ready answer for every question. He knew that everyone trusted him, while he likely trusted no one. If his curated persona—eager employee, community benefactor, church school superintendent—lowered others' guards about what he was up to, he kept his razor-sharp eyes focused on everyone around him. He was certain that on any given day he could be, and probably would be, found out.

That day nearly came after a string of rumors circulated outside the company suggesting that Geo. A. Hormel & Company was in financial straits because of its shortage of cash, prompting George to hire an auditor from Minneapolis to review the books. When the auditor arrived around noon, he requested to see the accounting records. Cy, who knew he was short $200,000 in company accounts that day, hemmed and hawed—then quickly came up with a plan that would provide respectable distraction for the auditor.

"I'm just in the midst of balancing the books," he claimed. "Why don't you go for lunch and a round of golf with Mr. Eberhart? I'll have the books ready for you on your return."

A few hours later—enough time for Cy to make *certain entries that placed the books above suspicion*, he'd later write—the examiner came back and found nothing amiss. Disaster averted.

I've wondered whether Cy latched onto A.L. that day simply because he happened to be in the office and anyone from Minneapolis would have enjoyed having lunch and a golf match with him, or if he had some other motive. I've also wondered what might have happened if Cy had never made that first theft by taking Mrs. Hollingshead's cash. If he hadn't, might he have risen legitimately to the position of comptroller, or even the equivalent of chief financial officer? He was smart enough. As George and A.L. enjoyed both the power and privilege of their positions, might Cy not have legitimately enjoyed his own? It's possible that, had he never stolen anything, the three men might have worked together for another twenty years, each accruing greater wealth and standing.

Later, while in prison, Cy would imply that he wrote his autobiography to dissuade other *callow youth* from following his path. I find some of his words nearly reasonable, even insightful, and he often comes across as a likeable person. I can see how he might have hoodwinked the company brass. But he also comes across as a manipulative liar. Which was truer? Maybe that first share of stock he purchased and later sold was not just an important totem for an innocent, upward-looking young man but a symbol of what he intended to do at the Hormel company from the start.

Cy claimed the only true, and greatest, harm he did in embezzling was to his wife, Maude, and their son, Gerld. But the truth is that he caused incalculable damage to George Hormel and to my grandfather, and his deeds nearly brought a thriving company to its knees.

13.

Tears in My Arugula

Austin

2000

Friday morning after breakfast at our hotel, Dikkon and I set off for our first appearance of the poetry celebration: an all-student assembly at Neveln Elementary School. There will be five more of these before the day is over.

"What do you think, Gretch?" my brother asks as we pull into the parking lot. "Maybe a hundred kids?"

The hollow gymnasium booms. At least five hundred yelling children are lined up in chairs, erupting in applause. It's deafening. The hardwood floor glistens. Thousands of poems have been collected and judged across Austin's schools, from kindergarten through high school, and the winning poems for each grade will be announced in our presence at school assemblies. After applauding the K–6 Neveln winners, we're swarmed by children—talking, touching, asking for autographs. I'm seduced by their young energy.

Kari Bain leads us to her fifth-grade class, where twenty children sit ready to ask us questions. Noticing the class is mostly Caucasian but with a sprinkling of Black and brown kids, I see Austin changing before my eyes. Five years ago, El and I saw no person of color anywhere we went. Now, these kids are widening the perspective in their classrooms around Austin.

Kari points us to two small seats in front of the room. The kids are alert and poised.

"Are you famous too?" a little girl asks me.

I smile. "No, just my dad."

"Does he still write poems?" one little boy calls out from the back left.

"In the middle of the night, sometimes, but it's hard to read his handwriting now."

"How many pencils did he use?"

I love this question. Dikkon takes it.

"A lot," he says, "but mostly ballpoint pens and his Smith Corona typewriter."

"How do you start a poem?" This one comes from a boy in a bright yellow shirt with a curly hair cut.

"I've only written a few," I toss out. "I think you start with a feeling or an observation, maybe something that interests you. Then you see where the words take you and keep working on each one until you get them just how you want them."

"What did you eat for dinner?" asks a girl with a halo of thick brown tresses, keeping her arm in the air through my answer.

"My mother wasn't much of a cook," I say with a laugh. "She fried hamburgers or boiled hot dogs and frozen corn. Sometimes she'd heat up a can of baked beans. We ate Dinty Moore stew and Spam sandwiches because they come from Austin."

"Which poets did you like best?" a front-row boy with soft brown skin asks my brother.

We were primed that the class has studied the poets of my father's generation, but still, I'm impressed.

"Robert Frost. Allen Ginsberg. Dylan Thomas. Robert Graves," Dikkon replies.

A half-generation younger than Dikkon, I overlap with him on some of those but also have a few of my own.

"When I was little, Robert Frost always struck me as kind of grumpy," I say.

A few kids grin.

"He was old, and I was younger than you the first time I met him," I go on. "He didn't seem too interested in little kids. But I liked his poems because I could understand them. I'll add to my brother's list Anne Sexton and Donald Hall."

"Which is your father's most famous poem?" The little girl who poses this question has eyes as blue as the sky outside the high windows of her classroom.

"Hm . . . 'The Groundhog,'" I say. "It's a long poem about finding a dead animal on a summer day and returning a year later to find its bones dried out—*beautiful as architecture.* I've always liked that phrase, *beautiful as architecture.* You might read it when you're in high school."

Suddenly, the kids are animated. "We've read it!" several call out.

My eyes widen. "Really?"

"Did you see the groundhog, too?" a little boy asks.

"No, just my dad."

"Did he really poke it?"

"Yes, I think he did."

A wiry boy sitting a few rows from us raises his hand. "I think the groundhog went to Heaven. I think he died, but his soul went."

With that, we're off on a spirited conversation about Heaven and groundhogs and the architecture of bones. I love these kids.

"Okay," Kari says, "let's have the last question."

There's a little girl to my right who's been quietly staring at me through the entire class. She flings her arm in the air, and I turn to her.

"Do you like your father?" she asks.

I'm tongue-tied. Not what I was expecting. No one's ever asked my opinion of my dad. And I know no one who *didn't* like him. I turn to Dikkon. "You go."

"Of course," Dikkon says. "I like him very much. I love my father."

"What about you?" the girl persists.

Her question deserves an answer, but I don't know what to say. I hesitate, then try to do her justice.

"There were amazing writers in our house—always," I say. "I don't think I know my father, and I don't think he knows me. Not like your dad probably knows you or like I know my kids."

I'm stalling. What should I say to this little girl with her tough question? My face flushes. My hands sweat. I'm here to celebrate my father. It would be easier to lie, but I've been doing that for too long.

"I like that my father is so generous to so many people, especially writers like you. I don't like that he found others more interesting than me." I look out at the children and wonder what they take in. "It's fun being here today. I've loved hearing my dad's stories about Austin."

I turn to the little girl. "And thank you for that question."

DIKKON DRIVES OUR GOLD VAN TO AUSTIN'S NEW restaurant, Chatham's, downtown. I'm quiet in the car, absorbing the fact that I didn't have an easy answer for the little girl and how much that says about my relationship with my father. It's broken, even if few in Austin know that, or need to know it. And I'm here to represent him.

Maybe Dikkon didn't notice my hesitation, as he doesn't mention it.

Seated in the middle of this busy restaurant, I eyeball the grilled veggie sandwich on the menu that comes with an arugula salad. Change has come to Austin's menus, too, since El and I were here and our only food choices were Hormel meats.

When the food comes, I scarf down my sandwich, leaving the arugula for last. The fifth grader's question has stirred me up.

"It bothers me that Dad is so revered here," I say.

"Why wouldn't he be? He came from here." Dikkon shrugs. "He's the most famous author Austin has produced."

"But if he cares about Austin, why hasn't he come back? Why didn't he ever bring us here?"

My father and mother did make one trip out here in 1971 when Dad was asked to speak to the senior high school class on the occasion of his fiftieth high school reunion. In his address, he took a strong stand against the war in Vietnam, imploring senior boys to refuse military service. According to Mom's journal from that trip, she was afraid he'd be booted out of town.

"I wish he'd brought us here," I say. "But how can they honor him when they don't even know him?"

"They think they know him. His fame makes them proud."

"It should make me proud. But it's all he cared about. He had no idea who I was. He still doesn't."

My brother lifts his eyebrows. He's quiet, while I'm just getting started.

"Dad had a *story* of me. But it wasn't me. When I was in fifth grade—like that little girl—you were at boarding school. When I was in high school, you were in college. Maybe you just missed the worst of it."

Tears fall in my arugula. I push away my plate and ask Dikkon to pick up our check. I need air. Outside, I feel adolescent, even embarrassed by my emotion. I hadn't a clue this trip would trigger how unresolved I am about Dad, nor how mixed up that lack of resolution is with understanding my grandparents. I need to get myself together. I watch cars pass, and think of something my kids say, no matter what kind of day they've had, before they take to the baseball diamond or lacrosse field: *Game time.*

I will say the right things here, but I'm tired of being my father's surrogate.

Waiting for Dikkon outside Chatham's, I want to have some fun this weekend. Today—the classrooms of kids, the poetry prize winners, being part of this citywide celebration—has been a roller coaster of emotions. Paralleling ones I have about my family—so much fun mixed up in secrets and denial. The rest of this weekend, I'll focus on fun.

14.

It Was the Sausage

Austin

1916–1920

Ever since 1891, when George Hormel opened his first meat market in Austin, he'd been making wet sausage. Made by stuffing highly seasoned waste from cuts of pork into the lining of a calf's stomach and then tying it off at the ends, the product provided a longer shelf life than fresh-cut meats.

Throughout Europe, wet sausage had long been known as a leveler, a product that could bridge people from times when fresh meats were plentiful to leaner times when they weren't. Its shelf life was further extended when spice caravans arrived in Europe from Asia. And as it became a food staple, every European country created its own flavor. It could be made from almost any part of an animal, and seasoned to taste.

Wet sausage had been a top-selling product for Geo. A. Hormel & Company from its start. And a savior. After the Financial Panic of 1893, when George was asked how his company had survived, he replied, "I think it was the sausage."

Dry sausage was a different product. It, too, was made of cast-off bits of meat, mixed with flavors, and pressed into casings, but unlike its wet sister, it required curing and drying before it could be sliced and diced and consumed without cooking. Easy to pack and carry, then sliced and eaten, it was perfect for salesmen like my grandfather, who frequently drove their automobiles or rode trains for long distances.

George wanted to create the perfect dry sausage and A.L. was eager to sell it. After experimenting with small batches, George made a strategic bet and formed a dry sausage division in 1915. He hired Walter Bergman, who hailed from a longtime sausage-making family in Iowa, to run the operation. Like his new boss, Bergman was a stickler for details. His goal was to produce enough dry sausage to meet the market needs of big East Coast cities. The first Hormel dry sausages were named Holsteiner, Cedar Cervelat, and Noxall Salami. Once the originals were perfected, Bergman and his team made links they called Di Lusso Genoa Salami and Marca La Parimissima Prosciutto. These were sold to the Italian markets in New York. For the Germans, Bergman created Thuringer. For the Swedes, it was Goteborg. In executing its brand strategy for innovative merchandising, the Hormel company was creating and exploiting market niches. During the first year of sausage sales under the new division, revenue hit $5 million.

New Americans arriving from Europe wanted their sausage to taste like the ones they'd left behind. The Hormel company would oblige, but dry sausage took months to make. A Di Lusso Genoa might hang in a drying room for 120 days to obtain its signature bloom, and during that time everything—room temperature, humidity, and airflow—had to be perfectly maintained.

Hormel pulled it off, and the company rapidly became known for having among the best dry sausages in the country. By the 1930s, the dry sausage division would offer thirty varieties; by 1950, it boasted 150, and was available worldwide. John Hormel's mantra, *Innovate, don't imitate*, was baked into Hormel's sausage formula and into the company's DNA. Sausage growth led to Hormel links taking up early shelf space in meat shops from Chicago to Brooklyn.

Where dry sausage needed no refrigeration, most Hormel products did. Every winter, the company hand-cut blocks of ice from the Cedar River and its employees carried the large bricks by hand or cart into factory rooms for storage. This approach worked until one year the Cedar River failed to freeze over, causing a crisis in refrigeration that forced George Hormel to buy his first ammonia compressor. After that, the company still cut ice but became less dependent on it.

LILLIAN BELLE GLEASON AND GEORGE HORMEL were married on February 24, 1892. Lillian, the daughter of New England farmers who had moved to Minnesota in the 1860s, had relocated from Blooming Prairie to teach in Austin's Franklin School. George met her as the organist for the Presbyterian church that he attended. She loved music and good books, as my grandmother did. After she married George, she paid cash for his meats at the provision market and kept the company's early books. As the company grew, she figured payroll, wrote ads, paid bills, and made up pricing lists, all the while running the Hormel household on a budget of thirty-five dollars per month.

In 1901, the year A.L. arrived in town, the company slaughtered over 32,000 hogs, and George and Lillian bought an Italianate mansion built of brick with Tuscan farmhouse influences at 208 4th Avenue NW. They invested $50,000 (about $1.7 million today) in renovations, stuccoing over the red brick exterior and painting the mansion a warm yellow.

Most of the building materials were shipped from Europe. To the front of the home, they added a two-story veranda. The veranda's roof was held up by soaring two-story columns shipped to Minnesota from Italy.

By 1916, Austin had a population of 9,000, with most residents owning their own homes. Brick-built businesses were taking the place of older wooden ones. An up-to-date courthouse had been completed for $15,000. Austin boasted five hotels, an adequate sewage system, and miles of broad, level streets made from cement. Its volunteer fire department coordinated forty-five men in two companies, and its public school system, which educated 1,300 students across six large buildings, was considered as good as any in the state. The city also had its own commercial school, which enrolled hundreds of students from across Minnesota and beyond for post–high school education in business. Like most company towns, the small city developed in lockstep with its signature, rising company.

IN 1914, GEORGE HORMEL WAS INVITED to Washington, DC, to hear food administrator Herbert Hoover's outline for wartime measures to regulate the country's meatpacking operations. Plans were to put meatpackers under government contract to conserve and increase the country's meat supply for the war effort and the burgeoning growth of the US population. The government hoped to stabilize prices and prevent packers from selling to retailers who could charge whatever they wanted. Through the next several years, Hormel company accounts would be audited by the federal government, which would also ascertain a fair cost of meat across the industry and make a "fair allowance" for company profits.

George liked Hoover. Partly influenced by his mother, who, back in Toledo, had eked out what little money possible so each of her children could have their own shoes, George believed in the communal good. He saw an important role for government, both locally and nationally, and admonished industrial leaders to take more responsibility in their own companies or risk greater regulation and intervention from the government. George believed some form of sharing was necessary for society to survive.

By the time of World War I, the Hormel company had weathered the 1907 depression, corn crop failures, cholera outbreaks in hogs, fire, and floods. More than 10 percent of its goods were being exported, and it would sell millions of pounds of meat in Europe in the years to come. But its men were headed off to war. It desperately needed to fill four hundred positions and turned, full-on, to hiring women. To help Austin families on Christmas Eve 1918, most of whom were missing the fathers of their families, George voluntarily cut electricity to the packing plant so that Austin women would have sufficient power to prepare proper holiday meals.

Despite the company's continued growth, not all went smoothly during this period. In 1915, a small group of employees tried, unsuccessfully, to establish a bargaining agreement with Hormel management. In 1917, one hundred workers walked off the job, setting off the company's first strike. Better wages were a concern, as were issues of steady work versus seasonal work. George agreed to some concessions, as he could see that political winds were shifting toward favoring labor.

Jay Hormel, twenty-two years old, became the first Minnesotan to volunteer for duty in World War I. He calculated that if he didn't, he'd be perceived as getting out of service because of his wealthy father, a perception he didn't want. Jay never saw battle while stationed in France, but he fell in love with a miller's daughter, Germaine Dubois, and brought her back to Austin in 1922. Together, they built their first home, which resembled a magnificent French chateau, and went on to raise three sons, George's grandsons: George II, Thomas, and James.

By 1919, the company's net sales revenues had tipped toward $30 million, and for the first time, it was processing over a half-million hogs. Following the annual stockholders meeting, A.L. was named second vice president, placing him in line for succession. Jay Hormel was named treasurer and given the job of overseeing all company finances, including the supervision of Cy Thomson.

As the company prospered, midwestern farmers began hinting at what they saw as a coming economic downturn. They would prove right. Between 1919 and 1929, farm income would fall from $22 billion to $13 billion, and the seeds for that decrease were felt at the Hormel company's twentieth anniversary. At the same time, a third of all wealth in the country was being earned by 5 percent of US residents. Most families were in debt. While the Hormel company grew, more than 60 percent of Americans lived just below the poverty line. Farmers, Black Americans, and immigrants were hit especially hard. Through the late 1910s, farmers had produced more crops than needed, which had led to falling prices and an increased need to borrow from banks to survive. Many farmers, ultimately, had to sell their farms or let them go.

Still, by the end of 1920, George Hormel likely saw himself on a safe plane: His family had grown, as he now had a daughter-in-law and his company was doing the best it ever had. Maybe, for the first time since leaving Toledo, he considered that all the risks he'd taken, pennies he'd pinched, and investments he'd made were paying off—for his family, the town, and the thousand workers under his employ. An immigrant entrepreneur had made it from nothing to build the start of a great American company.

ON MAY 24, 1915, A.L. PURCHASED A NEW HOME for his family on forty acres of land. Situated on the west side of Austin, the property included forty prime acres running north along the Cedar River. Witnesses to this occasion included Lena and the Hormel company's comptroller, E.S. Selby. A.L. immediately invested $50,000 in improvements, matching his boss. The eighteen-room house sat on flat land from which the Eberharts could see its twenty-acre apple orchard and the Hormel factory's signature smokestack across the river, billowing plumes of steam.

My grandfather named his estate Burr Oaks, after the trees along the river, though it was registered as Burr Oak Farm. The place was like a character on my family stage, a reference point for my father that he'd return to regularly in his stories. We knew its details—the veranda where Dad and Dryden hand-cranked ice cream on Sundays, its sitting room with a parlor piano around which the family gathered for song, its

custom-designed stained-glass windows, and its winding driveway edged with peonies. Little Elizabeth toddled after her mother as Lena tended its spreading perennial and rose gardens while its staff of cooks, housekeepers, and handymen tended the estate.

"Rows and rows of trees," my father would say about the orchard. "I'd lose myself in them. That orchard was fascinating, dense, wild, and full of adventure."

In the Burr Oaks basement, A.L. installed a full-size gymnasium for pickup basketball games with his children and their Austin friends. The room could be converted for balls and cotillions. George and Lillian Hormel would surely have been at some of those events—so too the Catherwoods, Adah and Ralph Crane, and the Selbys.

With his new title of executive vice president, his home renovations completed, and his growing portfolio of Hormel stock, A.L. turned to new forms of investing. His primary purchase was a 160-acre farm, complete with a milk house, silos, a double corncrib, and a bunkhouse, that he named Whispering Pines. It was there he founded the Minnesota

Holstein Company, for the purpose of raising best-of-breed Holstein cattle. He began with a herd of ninety dairy cows, and hired a staff to care for and milk them four times a day.

Vern Culver was hired as farm manager, Von Drum as dairy herdsman, and F. J. Gerlach as his field manager. Along with day and night milkers, A.L. added to his stock a group of Holstein bulls and purebred Duroc hogs—the same hogs Cy Thomson was raising at his farm down the road in Blooming Prairie. My grandfather also kept eight horses and several sulkies for racing. And as did George, A.L. paid above-average salaries.

As his livestock herd grew, A.L. entered his animals in judging competitions and began taking home prizes. At one time he owned the best butter-producing cow in the United States.

It's hard to imagine that George Hormel wouldn't have viewed all this extracurricular activity as a conflict. Maybe he reasoned that he'd hired an ambitious man and admired A.L.'s entrepreneurial spirit. He certainly couldn't complain about A.L.'s results for the company—a twenty-year run of year-after-year growth in sales. I prefer to think that George liked my grandfather as much as everyone did, though I wonder if he showed it. And neither Cy nor my grandfather was alone in their side investments. W.W. Walker, president of Farmers & Merchants State Bank of Austin, one of the company's primary sources of credit, also raised a livestock herd on the side of his bank employment. Ella Marie had told me as much at the historical society.

Still curious, I repeated this question about what George might have thought of my grandfather's Holstein herd to Ella Marie by letter. She didn't disagree that A.L. would have mostly been admired for his livestock.

"Cattle and hogs and farming, that's what you did in southern Minnesota," Ella Marie wrote.

When Dryden and Dick were sixteen and fourteen,

respectively, A.L. put them to work at Whispering Pines during its second summer season. They bunked with the workers for a month while Lena and Elizabeth visited her family in White Hall. He needed to keep his boys busy, and they could use their earnings for something for themselves.

On June 19, A.L. dictated a letter to his sons, letting them know he'd pick them up for *a vacation trip—some at our house—some up in the Indian country—then you'll work in the [Hormel] office or the plant for the rest of the summer. I think then you will be in fine shape for school.* He expressed a hope that they weren't too homesick and warned, *Be very careful about machinery, bulls, and strange horses that kick. Watch your health closely and try and make yourself useful so that Mr. Culver can afford to pay you something.*

A.L. had three primary values with which he raised his children, ones my cousins and I also heard about when we were kids. *Health. Honesty. Hard Work.* His list always started with health. Without that, you'd have nothing. Plenty of fresh air, athletics, good food, and rest made up his definition of maintaining one's health. Honesty came next. A.L. professed no room for cutting corners, no room for lying about schoolwork or skipping chores. If you weren't honest, he counseled his children, you couldn't be trusted. Finally was Hard Work. He expected this of both boys and Elizabeth. By the age of twelve, the boys had summer jobs and Elizabeth had household chores to help the family. A successful man or woman was healthy, honest, and a hard worker. Every letter A.L. wrote to his children reminded them of these three essential qualities. In addition, as his children became adults, he'd admonish them with these values and to follow the laws of any state or country they visited.

That summer, my grandfather concluded his letter to his boys with company news: *Very busy and expect Mr. Cassell of*

Baltimore and Mr. Bischoff from St. Louis to be here Thursday or Friday. Expect to have them up to the house. As ever your devoted father, A.L. Eberhart.

JUST AS GEORGE HAD BEEN IN 1914, A.L. WAS called to Washington by Herbert Hoover after the war, in 1918. Joined by a dozen top executives from an array of US industries, A.L. was instrumental in organizing the American Provisions Export Company (called APEC), a consortium of US industry representatives who would spend six months assisting European countries in reestablishing their own markets and importing US products after the devastation of war. My grandfather counted this work among his top lifetime achievements. It signified, above all else, his desire to bring together men from different backgrounds, places, and industries, and his commitment to serve our European allies in need. On his return home, he brought a few material rewards to share with his family—a French bracelet for Lena, Swiss watches for Dryden and Dick, and a doll from each country he'd been in for Elizabeth.

IN MID-SEPTEMBER 1920, THE MINNESOTA Holstein Company took home all the big cattle prizes at the Minnesota State Fair, including four firsts and three seconds—more than any other breeder or combination of breeders in the state. The event was the greatest exhibition of Holstein cattle ever shown in the history of the Minnesota State Fair.

That A.L.'s two-year-old company showed well against herds owned by men who had been in the business for years was pointed out in newspaper accounts, especially since his was the first herd of all-registered Holsteins in the county.

The success that has been attained by the Minnesota Holstein Company has been phenomenal, enthused the *Austin Weekly Herald* on September 15, 1920. These winnings brought national attention to A.L.'s company—and as his breeding stock grew, he helped organize the Mower County Holstein Breeders Association, which met regularly at the Fox Hotel in Austin. On January 21, 1921, twenty-five breeders were entertained by A.L. Eberhart, Vern Culver, and W.W. Walker, president of Farmers & Merchants State Bank. A.L. predicted that Mower County would become the greatest Holstein breeding center in the country.

Sometimes, A.L. would secure a loan from a bank—whether he really needed to or not is a question—to buy a new car, invest in a pedigree bull, or develop his farm. Bankers were eager to supply his needs. His payments were timely, his character top-shelf. Based on my grandfather's letters, there seems to have been a more casual lending system, too, between individuals. Breeders and brokers would loan money to each other and seal their agreements by a handshake or a simple IOU scratched out on a piece of paper, perhaps over a bourbon in a hotel bar or a cigar on a golf course. I found among my grandfather's papers reference to plenty of friends to and from whom he had loaned and borrowed money, mostly in sums of tens to a hundred dollars.

WHILE A.L. WAS BUSY SUSTAINING RECORD sales at the Hormel company and raising his prize-winning cattle, Lena focused on raising her children and creating better conditions for the people of Austin. On November 17, 1920, she helped organize the city's first well-child clinic, staffed by a county nurse and pediatrician from the University of Minnesota, in Minneapolis. The *Mower County News* wrote that *class distinction and financial rating will be forgotten at the initial baby clinic—it is for rich and poor alike*. Lena hoped the clinic would be made permanent, and she personally canvassed Austin neighborhoods to invite families to attend.

In June of that year, on a cool enough day in Austin to warrant a fire in her drawing room, Lena and her best friend Adah Crane entertained twenty-five women at a luncheon at Burr Oaks. As my father would tell me, these gatherings were both social and philanthropic. Any woman married to an influential man was invited to become a member of the Austin Floral Club, one of the first of its kind in the country.

A different form of entertainment and education at Burr Oaks came from my father's and Dryden's membership in the Duodecim Literary Society. Formed in 1903 as a branch of the national group, the Duo's purpose was to ensure twelve chosen young men gained skill and experience in public speaking and Robert's Rules of Order. The meetings rotated between the homes of its members. In their respective senior years of high school, both Dryden and Dick served as president. After its formal meetings, the Duos were treated to a dinner prepared by the boy's mother. Lena frequently accommodated these events, as did Lillian Hormel when her son Jay was a Duo.

Occasionally, Lena hosted purely social gatherings for the Duos; one evening, for example, the members and their lady friends assembled for an informal party of cards and pool in the basement gymnasium, converted to a dance hall and decorated in Halloween colors. The Duodecim Society's year ended with an annual banquet, and Lena frequently hosted it at Burr Oaks. This club, for boys only, was one way young men of Austin were enculturated to a life of expectation and privilege.

ON THE SAME DAY AS AUSTIN'S FIRST WELL-CHILD clinic, the Holstein-Friesian Breeders Association of Mower County held its first annual sale and offered up forty head of cattle. Whispering Pines counted for six of the sales, garnering $2,892 in total (about $47,000 today), and the highest-priced animal at the sale was A.L.'s at $615 (about $10,000 today). By then my grandfather was driving a Cadillac Suburban and his net assets had topped $500,000 (nearly $8 million today). At forty-four, he probably felt like he was ringing the bell on Wall Street and that things would only go up from there. The preacher's son had made it to the top of his field.

My father used to say that his family symbolized the best of all that was possible in America at the time. And while a company's success rarely repeats itself forever year over year, no one observing George Hormel or A.L. Eberhart, the Hormel company, or Austin in 1920, could have conceived of how quickly and disastrously that entire world would fall apart in the next twelve months.

15.

Power in Promotion

LeRoy, Minnesota

1915–1920

When Cy Thomson was eight years old, his father bought him a pony. The Thomson family owned little land, so to handle raising livestock they leased pasture from neighbors. Cy spent his childhood summers riding his pony bareback and herding his father's young calves between pastures. He bathed and brushed his horse, entered it in fairs, became conversant in pony bloodlines, and learned the best cattle brands for meat and milk, as well as the diseases that afflicted farm animals and the ages at which they were most susceptible to them. If he thought ahead, he might have considered he was setting himself up for his anticipated life as a farm laborer.

After purchasing back his family's small farm in LeRoy and establishing the buildings that would comprise his Oak Dale Farms, Cy went bigger, turning it into Oak Dale Farms and Amusement Park. As he kept up his stealing, he maintained the story that he'd earned the money with prudent investments in the stock market. Still, anxiety threatened to bury him. *I laid awake nights juggling columns of figures in my head*, he'd later write, *balancing ledgers which could never be balanced without knowledge of the peculations which I, alone, knew. And I had the details for my own farm business to remember too.*

With increased takings, Cy purchased a second property outside Blooming Prairie, northwest of Austin, not far from my grandfather's Minnesota Holstein Company. The 160-acre lowland plot, with a puny grove of trees and no buildings, provided the canvas for his second farm, this one for Holstein cattle and Duroc hogs. Over the next three years, he built what he claimed to be a $300,000 (about $4.8 million today) herd of Holsteins. His cattle barns were equipped to suck the ubiquitous flies into a killing chamber. His swine barns were steam heated. His enterprise became known as *a hired man's heaven*, where his help slept in dormitory rooms with freshly laundered linens, rugs, and drapes rather than on hay bales in the barn.

Next, he started Oak Dale Grain Farm right in Austin, to grow the crops he needed to feed his animals. Nearby, also in Austin, he set up his business office. His burgeoning enterprise was overseen by a board of four men, with Cy as chair. Howard Goss was the company's president. The company's offices included a stenographer's room, with a dozen women keeping up the correspondence, and a full-scale mail room, simulating Hormel's setup. A reporter for *Farm Mechanics Magazine* who arrived in Austin to investigate Oak Dale Farms was smitten with how modern and well-constructed the farms were. He noted the sleek look of the administrative offices, especially, and that everyone he met, *from the brakeman on the train to the president of the bank, enjoyed Cy's personality.* The author wondered how any person could find the time to run these three businesses while serving as full-time comptroller at the Hormel company, but like everyone else, Cy seduced him with his charm and his considerable capability. The author wrote it was only a tireless worker who could possibly do so much. Cy Thomson, he wrote, was that.

In his autobiography, Cy claims that his primary ambition for stealing Hormel funds was for *promotion and more power in the company*. He might have been a "cyclone" of a boy, but he shared a truth with George Hormel: he'd grown up poor. Money was important, but, for Cy, it wasn't the money itself so much as it was what the money brought with it. Saving held little interest for him. He stole to build a reputation that would afford him admiration and access to power.

With every promotion at the Hormel company, and with every addition to his farms in LeRoy, Blooming Prairie, and Austin, Cy was seen as far more than the simple farm boy he'd been as a kid. He bought a stately home for his family, not unlike the ones that George and A.L. had. His simple salary at Geo. A. Hormel & Company never could have achieved him these goals, but the company was awash in cash and Cy knew where to find it. He knew when it arrived and when it departed. He knew the company's bankers. When he started taking money, he probably figured a little wouldn't be missed, at least not immediately. But by 1915, it was no longer a little.

AFTER A LONG, FROZEN MINNESOTA WINTER, summer arrived, and Cy and Maude moved their family from Austin to LeRoy so Cy could oversee his burgeoning enterprise there. However, he needed to be in Austin by seven thirty every morning to read the Hormel mail and cover his tracks. That was sixty miles by car. *I had little time to eat. I scarcely slept*, he'd write. *It was a devil-driven life.* He sold his first car and bought a better one, then traded that for an even newer one that could shave ten minutes off his commute. By this point, every second counted.

George Hormel admired Cy for his efficiency, not knowing that he was plying that skill primarily to protect his embezzling. Cy was always looking for small fixes, just as his boss had in his early years, reinventing every kill and cut of a hog. Perhaps this is why Thomson would later claim that he never felt under any significant suspicion through the first five years of stealing. It was only after ratcheting up his take that he did—though even then, all company executives were focused on sustaining year-after-year growth while building their brand in the marketplace, and didn't seem to be paying much notice to Cy.

In 1917, the Austin guardsmen were called up to St. Paul to protect against a streetcar strike. Cy's poultry farm manager was in New York attending an educational session on new practices for managing stock birds. Cy used his employee's absence as an excuse to get out of militia duty. In truth, he couldn't afford to be away from his farm in LeRoy, or his job in Austin. By then he'd shorted the company $30,000, and if he sold everything he then owned, he figured he might just be able to cover it. He even reasoned that he could admit to his cheating, and though he would likely be fired, he'd at least be even with his boss.

Instead, he amped it up. In 1917, he took $28,000. In 1918, he took $88,000. Between November 1920 and July 1921, he stole a whopping $606,000 (nearly $11.3 million today), roughly half of his entire embezzlement.

EVENTUALLY, AFTER HEARING TOO MUCH ABOUT Cy's real estate and livestock developments, George brought him into his office for a chat.

"Maybe you should give up your job and devote yourself to your farms," George suggested, inviting such an outcome.

"Isn't my work satisfactory?" Cy asked.

"Yes, it is, but I wonder how long you can continue to divide your attention."

"Nothing is more important to me than my job here," Cy declared. "I'm just a stockholder of the farms. My cousin operates them."

George believed him.

IN 1918, WHILE A.L. WAS AWAY FOR SIX MONTHS in Europe, records suggest that Jay Hormel first became Cy's supervisor. It was during this time that Cy turned up the embezzling spigot and trained his sights back on LeRoy. It's hard to tell whether he envisioned this hybrid county farm/amusement park as a whole, or if it evolved like a fever as he took more and more money and needed to do something with it. Whatever his motivations, it became the largest amusement park west of Chicago, a kind of forerunner to Disneyland.

Cy laid in a public swimming pool, the largest of its kind in the entire region. He installed a ten-acre playground for children. He built a baseball diamond and invited precursor teams to the minor leagues to play ball. To transport feed from feed rooms into his barns, he installed overhead tracks. As thousands of cars came to his amusement park and traffic piled up on the highway in each direction, he installed a tunnel under the road opening into the basements of buildings on each side so his help could efficiently move from one side of the campus to the other despite the crowds. No idea of his went unfunded.

On August 10, 1919, Oak Dale Farms and Amusement Park pulled in a whopping sixty thousand people. So many vehicles—eight thousand automobiles piled in, along with railroad cars, jitneys, buggies, wagons, and trucks—that the park had to procure space from neighboring farms and school yards. It was advertised as the "largest poultry exhibition ever staged." Behind glass doors and windows, visitors watched twelve hundred chicks peck their way to freedom. Exhibition air flights did loop-the-loops, tail spins, and spiral dives. The Hormel Men's Club Band entertained spectators. Poultry experts were impressed; H.A. Nourse, publisher of *Poultry World* in St. Paul, said, *The astounding demonstration here today is by all odds the greatest and most stupendous ever staged by a poultry man anywhere in this country. Mr. Thomson is doing more for the improvement of poultry raising than any other individual in the United States today.*

Not to be missed in the exhibitors' pavilion was a large layout of products from Geo. A. Hormel & Company.

TO PROTECT HIS PROPERTY IN LEROY, CY BUILT a firehouse and hired twenty full-time firefighters, where every other town had volunteers. People in LeRoy were ecstatic. Cy was turning the town into a national destination.

Cy worked with railroad companies to ensure Pullman cars would pick up his customers in Chicago on a Friday afternoon, dine and lodge them in sleeping compartments, and deliver them to LeRoy the next morning. After a weekend of baseball games, eating hot dogs and barbecued chicken, and swimming in the pool, parents could put their kids back on the Pullman and dance the night away at the dancing pavilion. On Sunday, they'd be delivered back to Chicago. Word spread fast of the fantastically good times being had at Oak Dale Farms and Amusement Park.

That one man could create so much for so many in such a short period of time is mind-boggling, even by today's thinking. Even with stolen money, this was a lot to imagine and execute. Cy was like a Minnesotan Jay Gatsby—the epitome of status, money, and class. Those in Austin and LeRoy with whom I spoke were simultaneously baffled by his audacity and awed by his inventiveness. He'd brought them glitz, splendor, and endless good times. At the end of a world war, what could have been better?

But it was a cynical creation. Made from new—stolen—money, taken from the real money that George Hormel and my grandfather, along with others, had been working hard to make. Cy pulled off his pleasure and greed right under the noses of the best auditors, and some of the smartest executives, in the country.

We cling to our myths, especially heady and intoxicating ones. We want to believe them as truth. We help in their construction by denying what's in front of us and filling in holes to reinforce their validity. And in every great myth there are heroes, ones we don't want to see fail. We want our town, our company, our marriage, our family, to rise and succeed, no matter what it looks like behind the veil. Cy created these myths, weaving himself into southern Minnesota's psyche like a boll weevil through a crop of cotton. By the time he was found out, it was nearly too late.

IN EARLY 1921, CY INVITED A GROUP OF STATE officials, legislators, and newspaper men to tour his park. The visitors sang the praises of the economic engine he'd created, bringing prosperity to Minnesota. When Cy excused himself before their meal was done, the visitors had no idea that he did so in order to rush back to Austin to intercept a query and send a telegram explaining why a certain deposit running into the hundreds of thousands of dollars hadn't reached a particular bank.

By then, he was in for over a million. He'd been promoted to the top financial position in the company and held the company's purse in his hands.

According to Cy, in the fall of 1920, George Hormel had received an attractive offer to sell his company (neither Hormel's autobiography nor the two Hormel company history books speak of this) and sent for Ernst & Ernst, the best accounting firm in the country. Founded in 1903 by Cleveland brothers, Ernst & Ernst had been in the business for seventeen years and was one of the largest firms in the country. (Today called EY after a series of mergers with other financial firms, it offers professional services globally from its headquarters in London. Along with Deloitte, KPMG, and PricewaterhouseCoopers, EY is one of the Big Four accounting firms remaining in the US.)

The Ernst brothers scrutinized Hormel's accounting records but found nothing out of order. The reassurance only emboldened Cy.

In March 1921, the *Minneapolis Tribune* reported that Cy's prize cow, a black-and-white Holstein named Bossie, was the welcome guest of honor at a banquet for 150 livestock breeders of Mower County at Cy's farm in Blooming Prairie. *After drinking her milk and eating her butter*, the reporter gushed, *guests eulogized Bossie as the greatest friend of the farmer in Minnesota.*

The Minnesota Good Roads commissioner was speaker at that banquet, and twenty-four guests from the Twin Cities attended. Also present was my grandfather and his (and George Hormel's) banker and breeder friend, W.W. Walker. Over dinner, Senator J. M. Hackney, of St. Paul, quipped to the crowd, *The average dairy cow now produces 150 pounds of butter a year. If this can be increased by one pound per year per cow, it will earn an extra $500,000 for farmers of this state. If it is increased by ten pounds, it will mean $5 million more.* Minnesota held all records for butter and milk production. Hackney concluded that Mower County was now the greatest dairy center in the country—just as A.L. had predicted it would be.

It was Ella Marie Lausen who, in 1997, first showed me this article from the *Minneapolis Tribune. Of course, A.L. would have been there*, I thought then, but a voice still nagged in my head: *If A.L. was there, then he and Cy were in the same room, not just on Hormel turf but also directly through their breeding interests.* They may not have been "in cahoots," as V. had suggested to El and me in 1995, but they were eagerly building their own brands and competing side by side for best-in-breed awards at fairs. And with W.W. Walker, the Hormel company's primary banker in Austin, also a part of the mix, it was all looking pretty cozy.

Still, I reasoned, *that doesn't mean my grandfather knew anything about Cy's embezzling.*

By the beginning of 1921, Cy Thomson had realized his original dream—he'd traded a simple share of Hormel stock for a boatload of money and created for himself and tens of thousands of guests an attention-getting, award-winning, national-news-procuring enterprise that had made him well-known to Minnesota movers and shakers, including up to the governor. He'd gotten away with his stealing for nearly a decade and was poised to keep it going. He kept his vigilant eye on the behavior of the men around him while gnawing at his fingernails, hoping not to be caught. It must have been a cyclonic adrenaline junkie's favorite state of being.

16.

River Rambles with Knowles

Austin

2000

The Red Cedar River, named by the Meskwaki people for the red cedar trees surrounding it, originates in Sargent, Minnesota, twenty-five miles north of Austin, and empties into the Mississippi River at Muscatine, Iowa, two-hundred and twenty miles south. Frequently referred to without its first name, the Cedar River twists and turns like a snaking rope for 383 miles, making it a beautiful string of water. Gold was discovered here, which once attracted panners to Minnesota though little of substance was found. Clams were farmed in its waters for their freshwater pearls, and it served as a good location for early settlers to set up flour and sawmills.

The Old Mill Restaurant, where El and I ate lunch with Betty Catherwood, is located in one of those historic mills. In the mid-1800s, the Red Cedar River provided commercial transport from north to south, but it's also known for flooding. In 1993, it was responsible for Iowa's worst flood on record, inundating twelve hundred blocks of downtown Cedar Rapids. In 2008, twenty thousand people were evacuated from Cedar

Rapids when it flooded again. Austin has known floods as well, the worst of them in 2004 when the river crested at over twenty-five feet and four feet of water swamped Main Street.

Many of my father's favorite stories involved the Cedar River, but I'll only ever know it as a lazy little piece of water on which I was lucky enough to enjoy some fun one afternoon in Austin.

WHEN THE ORGANIZING COMMITTEE FOR THE poetry celebration asked if there was anything special I'd like to add to our schedule, I emailed: *Get out on the Cedar River.* I had a specific destination in mind: to get upriver to Ramsey, where my father and Rog Catherwood camped out in 1919, two years before Cy Thomson's embezzlement was discovered.

Knowles Dougherty was game to help me and roped in Larry Dolphin, who runs the Jay C. Hormel Nature Center, so this morning Dikkon and I meet up with the two men at the center. Larry shows up with two canoes lashed to the bed of his pickup truck.

"Can we get to Ramsey?" I ask.

"If you're up to it," Knowles says. "It's a five-mile paddle."

I nod. "I'm up for it."

Knowles and I pair off in one canoe; Dikkon and Larry take the other. Knowles folds his long legs into the stern of our canoe and picks up his paddle while I sit on the bow thwart.

I'm ready for downtime and happy to see Knowles again. He and I have corresponded since I was last here, so I've gotten to know him fairly well. He knows of my ambivalence about Dad and has supported my quest to figure out what happened to my grandfather.

The river is low and dark with silt, more like a creek than a river, and its lack of water requires us to make frequent portages. It's nothing like the waterway I've imagined from

Dad's stories, nor the one I've read about in records of its flooding. We keep having to disembark and drag our canoe over logs, sandbars, and downed trees. Knowles is my perfect companion, as he's as insistent as I am on getting to Ramsey.

At one of the many Ys in the river, we become separated from Dikkon and Larry. By then, Knowles and I are a mile away from town in what feels like deep wilderness. It's warm and humid. The river is pungent as rust as we navigate mud flats and decaying leaves. I'm happy to be on the river with Knowles. I feel tied to my father's boyhood adventures—the idyllic part of his Austin stories.

A great blue heron flies overhead, pumping upriver, its wings thwapping ahead of us. Deer tracks punctuate the sandbanks on both sides. We make slow headway with portages, but the physical exertion and quiet beauty fill my spirit tank. I needed to return to myself after answering too many questions about my father by radio and newspaper reporters and smiling at TV cameras. Yesterday, I'd said I was proud of him, as they'd expected. I know I'll find my bearings in this quiet wilderness, no matter how imperfect a river day it is. It's hot and humid and sweat dampens my face.

"Do you want to go back?" Knowles asks at one more portage.

"No! I want to get to Ramsey!"

He and I toss conversation back and forth from bow to stern—about the celebratory weekend, about George Hormel's firing of my grandfather, about the subsequent loss of my grandparents' fortune.

"Remember what I told you the first time we met: George Hormel wasn't anything like your grandfather," Knowles says.

"How do you mean?"

"He was tough and demanding. He could be condescending to those less fortunate."

"Yes," I say, "and all his heirs are rich."

I can be honest with Knowles. From the beginning, he's consistently shared his opinion that my grandfather was wronged, but he also listens and wonders alongside me.

"I think you should sue them," he says.

This has never occurred to me. I turn my head around to face Knowles.

"You'd have to get a good lawyer. But you'd have a good case. You remember what Knowlton told me." Dick Knowlton, a recent CEO at Hormel, once intimated to Knowles that he, too, thought A.L. had been wronged. A month from now, Knowles will email me that he ran into Jim Holton, another recent CEO of the Hormel company, at a Rotary meeting and asked what he knew about George Hormel's firing of A.L. "Guilt by association only," Holton said. "Nothing more than that."

"Hmm," I say. "But your conversation with Knowlton was twenty years ago."

"They'd settle with you somehow."

"You mean for a lifetime supply of Spam?"

Knowles laughs and digs his paddle into the quiet water. "At the least they owe you an apology. Everyone knows your grandfather helped build that company."

"I still wonder what my grandfather knew," I share. "Thomson and A.L. were at the same livestock meetings. They competed for prizes at fairs. Thomson bought some of his cattle from A.L. Where'd that money come from?"

I look back at Knowles again and see he's taking this in.

"Anyway," I conclude, "I'm not in this for the money. It's just the more I hear, the more confused I am."

I settle into my thwart and breathe in the scent of dusky silt. I think about my father's journal from 1919, about his trip with Rog.

"Hey, you want to hear about my father's camping trip with Roger Catherwood?" I ask, changing the subject.

Knowles nods, so I stow my paddle and turn around while he keeps us moving upstream.

IT'S JULY 16, 1919, AND DAD AND ROG HAVE just finished a fortnight working in the Hormel plant. Rog has pocketed $12.40 for *stuffing George Hormel's sausages*. On payday, he and Dad sign a pact: *We solemnly set our autographs to the resolve to head up the Red Cedar River to the old campsite to explore the deserted habitation which sets far back from the railroad and east traffic road from Austin to Ramsey, Minnesota.*

That Saturday they shoulder packs full of camping gear and food, along with one rifle. The Eberhart family dog, Happy, follows close behind. The mid-summer sun is high, and my father's back aches under the weight of his provisions. Quickly drenched with sweat, the boys hike upriver for two hours, hacking back underbrush, crossing footbridges, and climbing over fences and logs. They arrive in Ramsey footsore and exhausted.

Their old campsite is just where they left it, next to a gooseberry sandbar on the east side of the river. The boys strip and dunk to cool off. They stow their jam and bacon

in the coldwater spring and hang their water bag from a tree. The tall wet grass teems with gigantic Minnesota mosquitoes that bite their bare backs *like hungry fish.*

Dad tries to make a fire to deter the bugs, but his matches are sodden with sweat and won't light, so he paces around concocting an alternate plan. Taking a piece of paper from his journal—I've seen the page he tore out, I say to Knowles—he lays it on his lap and empties gunpowder from his .44 shells on top, then piles a few wet, sweaty matches on for tinder. Then he places his makeshift bomb on the ground.

Standing back, he lifts his rifle and fires a direct shot. A spark lights, but no flame.

He paces the campsite again and keeps trying. On his tenth point-blank try, the bomb turns to flame. *Ah, Fire, the age-old friend of man!* he writes in his journal.

"WE'VE GOT ANOTHER PORTAGE," KNOWLES says now, "then tell me the rest."

We heft the canoe over another group of fallen branches and settle back onto our thwarts.

WITH BACON SIZZLING IN A PAN OVER THE FIRE, Dad and Rog finish off a loaf of bread and a pile of hamburgers. At 10:00 p.m., Rog reminds Dad of their pact. The boys grab their rifle and a flashlight and *stalk out into a wilderness gloom* for the haunted house in Ramsey.

Happy protects their flanks. Locusts and crickets chirp around them, and fireflies blink through the fog. They stumble through calf-high, murky river water as mist rises. The fog clears and they use the stars to find a barbed wire fence. They tear a blaze from Dad's shirt to mark the fence for their return. After counting eleven posts, they turn a hard left, and dead ahead is the deserted house.

Cornstalks cast long shadows in the moonlight, and heat lightning flares the sky. A monstrous freight train, black as the night, slowly clunks by.

Rog pulls a package of Life Savers from his pocket, and the boys fortify their nerves before entering the pitch-black building. Dad holds the loaded rifle just over Rog's shoulder as they climb the narrow staircase and swing open a door. A musty smell suggests a tramp just hopped the passing train. In the beam of their flashlight, they catch sight of a bottle of whiskey under a straw bed and swoop it up for later.

I STOP TALKING TO THINK ABOUT MY FATHER'S adventures on this river. Those adventures were passed down to me during my childhood and adolescent summers in Maine. Happy days on small sailboats on Penobscot Bay and camping on islands with friends. Digging for clams to steam for dinner, skinny-dipping in the dark, lying out under the stars in sleeping bags. Like the Cedar River's slow course through Minnesota to Iowa, this legacy wound through A.L. and my father, and took up in me. Our familial love of being in the outdoors with friends through three generations. And with my own children, a fourth.

I conclude the story for Knowles with the boys back at their camp, stoking their fire and trading opinions about the whiskey and the platform of the 1920 Democratic National Convention. By the light of their fire and deep into the night, Dad wrote in his journal, *We visited the deserted habitation in the darkness of night and kept to our word written in the pact! This is the LIFE!*

"Great story." Knowles smiles. "You've brought me back to that time."

"See why I wanted to get out on this river?"

"Not the best day for it, I wager."

"But we did it."

I pick up my paddle and turn toward the bow.

Just then, Knowles steers us up to a sandbank, and I know it's the one, the same gooseberry sandbar Dad described in his journal—on our right, the east side of the river, a gooseberry bush at its edge. I look up and see we're also at the golf course in Ramsey.

Knowles and I swat away a few mosquitoes, as Dad and Rog did eighty years ago.

"But the river is so much smaller than it was in my father's stories," I say.

Knowles nods. "Especially this year. We're in a drought."

It took us ninety minutes to paddle up to Ramsey, and in those ninety minutes I've reclaimed a part of my father I love, a part he inherited from his own father. My friend Knowles has given me a sanity break from this long weekend, and a memory I'll savor.

"I wonder what happened to Dikkon," I say, then see Larry and him walking down the sloping hill below the golf course to the river.

It turns out they turned back long ago, at the Y where we lost them—too many portages, they decided.

Knowles invites us all for a drink at the clubhouse.

In the clubhouse, I take a slug of my beer and glance at the bar TV overhead. It shows a 6:00 p.m. news lead about my brother and me and the what, when, and why of us being here to represent our father in Austin.

17.

The Jig Is Up

Austin

1921

On a warm, sun-filled day in the summer of 1921, Jay Hormel and his wife, Germaine, invited friends to join them for a drive to Oak Dale Farms. Jay, who now held overall responsibility for Hormel's finances, had been to his friend Cy's place before, but perhaps not in a while. He and his father had wondered about Cy's enterprise, given all the hoopla they'd been hearing about it, rumors flying around Austin like billiard balls on a felted table. Maybe just gossip, George thought, probably exaggerated in people's minds. He figured Cy's farms were making good money and it was being plowed back in—good for him.

That day, however, perhaps something didn't sit quite right for Jay. A gut feeling. Or maybe he just wanted to see the place again and it was a pleasant day for a drive. I imagine Jay and his wife dressed in their finest Saturday clothes—he in a fine suit, Germaine in a hat with streamers. It was a rare day off for Jay, who spent nearly every hour at the factory. I imagine him holding the car door for his wife as a mild breeze caught her silk scarf, sending it fluttering in the wind like the tail of a kite. They picked up their friends and headed south to LeRoy, the scent of green grass catching their breath.

The last twelve months had not been easy for the company. Hog prices were steeply down and Hormel, like other meatpackers with excess inventory, had been hit hard. Downgrading inventory meant a blow to the company's balance sheet. For the first time, sales were down too, and the US stock market was tapping its brakes. Company cash had been tight lately. But even with $3 million owed to all of its bankers and a yet-to-be discovered embezzlement whispering from the sidelines, George Hormel did not seem much concerned. Technically, the company was still growing its innovations and product line, and no bankers or auditors had brought up concerns about its accounts. When George asked Ernst & Ernst to specifically look into the company's cash shortage, they'd assured him, "If there's anything wrong, we'll find it. We consider a man a horse thief until we can prove him honest." They turned up nothing, though a half-million dollars had already been plucked from the company coffers by Cy Thomson.

At twenty-nine, maybe Jay wasn't fully reassured by the auditors' remarks. Maybe he couldn't shake the dissonance between the company's cash depletion and the rumors about Cy's ever-expanding businesses. Jay never had been the stickler for details that his father was, so maybe he simply trusted his gut more than George did, but his future was tied to Austin and he was heir to the company. He wanted to see Oak Dale Farms and Amusement Park again for himself.

ARRIVING IN LEROY, THE TWO COUPLES WOULD have stepped out of Jay's car into a sea of automobiles in what looked like a grand parking lot extending across flat prairie land. Throngs of visitors were filling the fields. Barns, stables, chicken houses, and a dancing pavilion were laid out around the property like a tidy campus with an open quad—not unlike the one Jay had known at Princeton, only built of farm-style white clapboard instead of Gothic stone.

I imagine Jay tallying as he strolled, with Germaine on his arm: landscaping newly installed next to wide pathways accommodating children running to and from the immense playground across the way; every building immaculately clean; workers' bunkrooms plush with comforts—mattresses and woolen blankets, drapes, a billiard room; the dancing pavilion, the largest in Jay's home state, graced with a shimmering hardwood floor and two thousand electric light bulbs. The barns didn't reek of manure. There was no blood or guts visible, no lard buckets, no urine-smelling chicken waste, no manure piles or rusting farm equipment. Was this a farm? Or a spectacle of sparkling agrarian entertainment—pure, beautiful fun that had sprung up nearly overnight like some futuristic movie set?

Was Jay struck by the ingenuity of it all? Did he remark on that to his wife and friends? Why *wouldn't* thousands of people come to LeRoy? Cy had created something unique— and in an outpost of southern Minnesota, far from the cities where you might expect it to be.

No matter what Jay thought of the place, he must have wondered above all, *Where did all the money come from?*

BACK IN AUSTIN, JAY RETURNED TO THE FACTORY, so it wasn't until the following Saturday, July 9—and then only by fluke—that he left the plant to find some operating numbers over in the accounting department at company headquarters. It must have been a rare moment when Ransome J. Thomson wasn't present. Jay perused the day's records, and one document caught his eye: the phrase "transfer of funds" was marked on a canceled Hormel company check, payable to Farmers & Merchants State Bank for $5,000 but credited to Oak Dale

Farms. His stomach lurched. Farmers & Merchants was the Austin bank whose president, W.W. Walker, was also a livestock breeder and had long been a primary local bank for the Hormel company. How could this be?

Jay collected H.H. (Tim) Corey at his home and briefed him on what he'd found. Corey, a big, beefy man, had been a good student and all-American football standout at the University of Nebraska before serving as captain on the front lines in France in World War I. He'd seen war in a way Jay had not. He'd also been a diplomat for the World War Peace Conference in Paris until 1919.

A year earlier, Corey had been in Austin visiting his friend Richard Banfield, also a friend of Jay's, and that's how the two had met. The Banfield family was equally close friends with the Eberharts. Corey, then heaving hog hindquarters in the Omaha stockyards, looked like he'd bring the "right stuff" to the Hormel company.

Like Cy in an early job with the company, Corey got his start at Hormel in the time department, cutting checks for employees while recruiting bright Nebraskans to follow him to Austin. His reputation for *hard, steady, uncompromising work* would follow him through the years to a job heading up its packing division. And, like Cy, Corey never took vacations.

In this moment, Jay wanted no one more than Tim Corey next to him while figuring out what was going on. The two headed over to George Hormel's home.

Maybe Jay tapped the horn of his car so as not to disturb his mother while attracting his father outside. This was a very delicate matter. If the situation was as bad as he thought it might be, it could ruin the company, would be a personal afront to George, and was likely to make national news.

Jay gestured for his father to come off the veranda, closer to him and Corey. What he'd feared had been going on, he told George, probably was. He referenced the check he'd found, stumbling over his words. Based on his quick scan through the accounting records (and perhaps coupled with what he'd seen the prior weekend in LeRoy), he feared Cy might have stolen a lot of money.

"It surely won't be anything too great," George said, unconvinced, reassuring his son. Maybe $100,000 at worst?

Jay and Tim Corey headed back to the company to find out. Behind locked and guarded doors, presumably to prevent Cy from entering the building, the men worked late into the night. Between January 1 and July 9, 1921, they discovered, nearly half a million dollars had been siphoned off Hormel company books and poured into the account for Oak Dale Farms at Farmers & Merchants National Bank. They assumed more must have been taken in prior years but couldn't take the time right then to figure it out.

AT SIX THE NEXT MORNING, JAY CALLED W.W. WALKER, at Farmers & Merchants, and requested that he meet them at his bank.

Displeased at being risen at dawn on the weekend, Walker questioned the urgent need for such a meeting.

"Problematic financial matters have arisen," Jay said, "that involve your bank."

The bank president resisted again.

"If you don't get to the bank immediately," Jay said, "I'll send for the sheriff to escort you."

At the bank, Jay asked Walker to produce every deposit slip for Oak Dale Farms that he'd received from January 1 to July 9. Itemizing and summarizing the total of these deposits, Walker came to the same $480,000 (nearly $7.5 million today) that Jay and Corey had tallied in the company's accounting department records, representing what would be the first half of money stolen.

It was true. There was no more denying it.

AT NOON THAT DAY, JAY CALLED E.S. SELBY, PRIOR comptroller for the Hormel company—the one Cy had recently replaced, who had also been a signer of A.L.'s deed for Burr Oaks. Selby then lived in Mason City, Iowa, but he drove the fifty miles to Austin immediately. When shown the incontrovertible evidence of Thomson's embezzling, Selby couldn't speak. Eventually, he mumbled something about Ernst & Ernst having gone over the books twice in the same year. It was impossible that any such defalcation of that scale could have taken place.

Jay knew otherwise. Back at his father's home, he said plainly, "I think we're broke."

According to George Hormel's autobiography, it was he who called Cy into his private office. This record matches the company's official history, which states that Cy spent two hours denying all charges before finally admitting to his guilt. Cy tallied a full list of his homes, farms, livestock, and equipment and told George that his thievery had started back in 1915, though many sources suggest it got started closer to 1910. Back in the time department, Cy had been responsible for keeping accurate hourly records for each employee. A company bookkeeper drew checks for the workers, but sometimes transient employees didn't pick them up, as they would quit after a single day of backbreaking packinghouse labor. Cy requested their checks be provided to him for cancelation; then he cashed them and pocketed their proceeds. It was shortly after this, sources suggest, that he took the more significant $800 in cash from Mrs. Hollingshead of South Dakota.

Cy's version of his firing differs from George's. According to his autobiography, on April 29, six weeks prior to Jay Hormel's trip to Oak Dale Farms, he received a letter from National Shawmut Bank of Boston demanding an analysis of the company's cash balance, to which he responded sufficiently to temporarily *soothe their feelings*. But Boston banking officials remained suspicious, he wrote, and in early July the Shawmut bankers corresponded with George directly, demanding a thorough investigation of the company's books. Maybe Cy had an inkling of what might come down.

On July 9, Cy claimed, George Hormel summoned him to the directors' room—not to George's office—where he found all directors of the company waiting for him. If true, then my grandfather was at the meeting, something I believe my father noted too. Cy knew he was in the red for over a million dollars and was about to be exposed. Walking from his office to the boardroom, he reassured himself over and over that he was not a criminal at heart. If he was, he surmised, he'd have the guts to lie again to his boss that day—which he didn't.

He claimed to have spoken first on arrival to the directors' room.

"Gentlemen," he said, "it's all over. The jig is up."

Cy had managed to convince the company's naive bankers, especially W.W. Walker, that Oak Dale Farms was a Geo. A. Hormel & Company concern. Transferring funds to Oak Dale Farms had therefore looked fine to the company's bankers, though none of them seem to have looked into the ruse over multiple years.

An hour after Cy's confession, company officials escorted him to the firm's general ledger where he made *the last entry [he] would*, charging himself, Ransome Josiah Thomson, with $1,187,000.

Cy wrote that he stayed at the company for an additional week to cooperate with outside accountants and bankers. *I was the most competent auditor of the bunch*, he said. *I knew where to look.* He traced every steal—where it had originated, where it had ended up—each data point kept in his head through nearly a decade. Based on the recommendation of his attorney, he transferred ownership of everything he owned in Minnesota and Iowa to the Hormel company. When he offered up his personal home, Hormel officers apparently refused to take it, presumably because it was all his wife, Maude, and son, Gerld, would be left with.

On Monday, a warrant was issued for Cy's arrest. Under concealed surveillance through the night and following morning, he was allowed to come to work, and it was there he was charged with grand larceny, handcuffed, and taken to the Mower County Jail. Jail accounts suggest he was a model inmate, as debonair and calm as he'd always been, passing his time playing handball with other prisoners.

On September 6, 1921, Cy Thomson pled guilty to grand larceny with Maude by his side and was sentenced to fifteen years at Stillwater prison, one hundred miles from Austin. He was thirty-five years old.

When asked repeatedly by the press and the Hormel company if there was anyone in on the deal with him, Cy told them, solidly, *No. I had no accomplice in any theft I ever made from the company.* Asked if anyone inside the company had aided him, he replied, *No, there was no intentional connivance* by anyone inside the company. George Hormel claimed the same in his autobiography.

Cy scoffed at the *official laxity* that had permitted one man to have so much power over company coffers. He also felt relief in finally having been exposed. *The calamity,* he wrote, *for which I had lain awake nights for ten years, which had held me an office slave who dared not be absent when a single mail delivery arrived, was over the moment I had my first confession to Mr. Hormel. I slept more lightly that night, I believe, which shows the private hell into which a man's own wrongdoing can plunge him.*

18.

Too Big to Fail

Chicago

1921

Immediately following the discovery, George Hormel called the president of First National Bank of Chicago and reported the facts. The company was in the hole for more than a million dollars. It owed a total of $3 million to banks from Austin to Chicago to Boston and could not pay off its loans.

First National was Hormel's primary creditor, and its president was definitive: he would call together a meeting of every bank involved and expect Hormel management to be present. That meeting, scheduled for July 20 in Chicago, would determine the company's fate.

Meanwhile, thick and fast as a sandstorm, rumors flew through Austin and LeRoy and to every corner of the nation. Cy had a lot of friends in Minnesota and far beyond, and George Hormel was admired but not necessarily loved. Most sympathized with Cy, believing he never could have overseen such an embezzlement on his own. Up and down Main Street, residents predicted he'd been made a scapegoat for someone higher up. Angry residents expressed alarm at the harm the company was causing him and his family.

"He put us on the map," LeRoy residents would have said.

At least one Austin resident likely railed, "He's been so generous—why, he helped my cousin last week."

The financial truth was blinding. It must have knocked the literal wind out of both George and Jay Hormel and the company's sails. The full value of embezzled funds was a huge sum—$1.187 million (nearly $18.7 million today)—and national news. The *New York Times* first reported, erroneously, *Admits $150,000: Controller of Minnesota Packing Company Confesses Defalcation.* Later, the paper had to revise its headline to *Report Shows Embezzler Got $1,187,000. Thomson Spent a Million Dollars on a Chicken Farm.*

An impressive 1,300 newspapers picked up the story.

The *St. Louis Tribune Post-Dispatch* ran with: *How $5000 Employee Juggled Firm's Millions.*

The *Pittsburgh Daily Headlight* wrote: *Friends Stick with Idol of Main Street.*

The *Boston Globe* used: *High-Flier in the Farming Game—Cy Thomson of Austin, Minnesota, Out-Ponzied Ponzi and Now He Is Arrested.*

Immediately, every Hormel company asset was frozen, and the value of its stock plummeted to close to zero. The company was in immediate default of its multiple loans to multiple banks. Its reputation was broken. This scandal would affect not just the Hormels, Eberharts, and Thomsons but also every person associated with the company—its suppliers and brokers; its drivers, meatcutters, and meatpackers; and its customers. Between rising waves of gossip, there were troughs of hushed silence in Austin. The atmosphere was charged.

ON JULY 19, JAY HORMEL, THEN TWENTY-EIGHT, and his father, George, sixty, were driven to the Milwaukee Railroad Station to board an overnight train for Chicago. Townspeople lined the platforms in *little knots*, understanding that the Chicago meeting would decide the fate of their town. Momentarily, George's spirits lifted when he saw this support outside his compartment window. He and Jay only hoped they'd survive their meeting with the bankers.

As George gazed out the window, something hit him: it wasn't "his" enterprise to save anymore, but one that belonged to everyone in Austin. *I understood, as never before*, he would later write, *the moral implications and responsibilities inherent in the control of goods-producing mechanisms—what went with the power and privilege of industrial leadership.* The initial impetus and driving force to start his company had been his alone, but the results could never be. Meatcutters and clerks, customers, livestock brokers, farmers, salesmen—they'd all made the company succeed. As Hormel scribed, *there'd be no results for the one without the many.*

All the more reason for Jay and him to be seized with worry. Everyone in Austin—including the city itself—depended on a good outcome for this meeting with the bankers. It was a pivotal moment in the company's twenty-year history. The banker committee decision would be binary: they could vote to liquidate all remaining company assets and take the chance they wouldn't be made whole for their loans, or they could allow the Hormel company to remain in business and hope to be paid fully, but only later. The first option was not a good solution; they'd be giving up real money they were owed. But the second option wasn't much better. Who knew if the company could pull this off? Of the $3 million the Hormel company owed to the banks—both large and small, local and national—more than a third of that sum had been leeched by Cy, and was perhaps gone forever. Who knew whether his assets could be liquidated in a real estate market in free fall—or, if they could be, how quickly?

George Hormel would have to admit to the banks that the company, for the first year in its twenty-year history, would be ending 1921 in the red by at least half a million dollars. He and his son were in the worst possible position to be meeting with these financiers.

ENTERING THE MEETING ROOM THE FOLLOWING DAY, George doubted their prospects were good. Everything around him was dark. Brown mahogany wainscoting cast a heavy gloom. Dark drapes hung next to small-paned windows. The heavy, bleak conference table that dominated the room was surrounded by a dozen men in gray and black suits seated as if at a funeral, their faces empty.

These bankers didn't like this meeting any more than the Hormel men did. Their banks were owed significant money. The boards of their banks were pressing them. Still, I'm sure there was no question for George and Jay Hormel who held the power in the room.

The meeting was already in session when the Hormels arrived. George was asked to make his statement. The big-framed German—hog butcher by physique, heritage, and temperament—rose from his chair. His presence would have dominated the room. He must have looked out at those men whose names he knew, whose banks had kept him going for years, who now held his fate in their hands, and wondered just how to paint them the true picture.

Leaders must rise to such a moment. You may know your key points, and the numbers by heart, but you can't read the emotion in the room until you're there, standing exposed in front of your judges. George would need to bring the right language, the right poetic metaphor, to make the perfect pitch. He would need to lean on his unquestionable strength—the strength that had assured clean, quality meat to his customers—to convince every banker present to make the right choice.

Perhaps more personally than he'd ever done at a convention, George described to these men in detail where he'd come from and what he'd put into practice at Hormel—the lesson from his father to innovate rather than imitate, the lessons from his mother about frugality and the common good. He invoked his memories of the teeming city of Toledo, his discovery of the beautiful, sloping prairies of southern Minnesota. He assured the bankers there were practices he'd refined for years—like double-checking the weight of hogs to be sure each farmer bringing livestock to his stockyard was paid exactly what he was owed, and double-checking outgoing customer orders to ensure every vendor was paid the same. He'd never *intentionally* left anything to chance. His company had strived for the highest quality and had guarded its reputation from the start. He evoked his first kitchen in Austin, where his loving wife, Lillian, had done the company's books near the fire, their only spot of warmth. He described his sales organization, led by Alpha LaRue Eberhart, and the sales team that had grown from three Hormel brothers on bicycles to a national network of men selling $30 million worth of goods a year with credit losses of less than $3,000. The company's accounts receivable were close to one hundred cents on the dollar. He told of steady growth, the company's sound inventory, productive buildings, and state-of-the-art equipment, its hardworking people. Ending with his foundational success with bacon and sausage, he had fans in the room; I suspect there wasn't a person there who hadn't partaken of his bacon or sausage. Some of those conservative bankers might have wished they could rise in applause.

George paused for a moment and caught his breath. The room was so quiet, he'd write later, he heard his own heart beating. But he wasn't done quite yet.

Starting up again, George predicted what would happen if the plant were to close. He drew a picture of a thousand employees losing their jobs, a high number of lost homes, the disappearance of a $1.5 million annual payroll and the impact of that rippling through the southern half of Minnesota. He predicted life savings lost, farmers out of business, hog brokers from Minnesota east to Boston and west to California feeling the squeeze on their own balance sheets.

"Consider this," he said. "If you liquidate the company, you may get half your investment, but people will lose and there will likely be a run on your banks. Your banks, too, may not survive."

He made his pitch: If the bankers would be kind enough to carry the company's indebtedness for two years at 7 percent interest per year, he would pull his company out of its plight, and they'd be made whole. For that privilege, George pledged everything he owned—his stock in the company, his home, his personal investments, his life insurance. For bankers, in addition to good collateral, there's nothing loved more dearly than a hefty personal guarantee. George laid himself and his family on the table.

After making his final plea, he sat down to listen to his bankers.

A somber silence followed. There was no right answer. There couldn't be. Each option carried incalculable risk. No one knew precisely how to gauge what might arise from either; it was pure speculation. Like entrepreneurship and banking, you use the tools and knowledge you have to speculate and then execute the hell of out of whatever decision you make, hoping to end up close. (With a little luck, better than close.) Maybe no one wanted to speak first. If a flash of sunlight hit the windows, I doubt anyone noticed. It remained a dark room with a dark mood and a dark prospect for each man present.

George's stomach must have been tied in knots as he waited for their decision. In that thirty-minute statement, he'd worked as hard as he'd ever worked cleaving hogs.

Finally, after an eternity, E.E. Brown, then vice president of Chicago's First National Bank and head of its legal department, stood. Founded in 1863, his bank had been a significant financier of the Civil War and had, just eight years prior to this meeting, become an original member of the Federal Reserve. J. P. Morgan and Marshall Field were two of its investors.

All eyes left George Hormel and focused on Brown.

"Gentlemen," he said, clearing his throat, enunciating each word, "I move that we grant the extension requested, and that we put the affairs of the company in the charge of a committee chosen from the members present."

George probably knew that was coming. He wouldn't have wanted to cede control, he'd have bridled against it, but it was inevitable in the situation and a normal course for banks to take when a big company went bad.

Brown's motion was voted up unanimously. So impressed were they, the bankers said, they'd throw in another million to Hormel's combined indebtedness to ensure the company had sufficient working capital to pull itself out of its mess in two years.

George Hormel had proved to his bankers, as CEOs have done in the years to follow, that this company—a small meat-packing factory in Austin, Minnesota—was too big to fail.

THE HORMEL MEN RETURNED FROM CHICAGO victorious, and the small city of Austin exhaled. Packinghouse workers would not lose their jobs. Families would not lose their homes. What meager savings some residents had in bank accounts could stay there, hedging against a future unseen adversary.

For a day or two in July 1921, the world shone brighter, looked cleaner, smelled sweeter. Elbow room had blown in from Chicago on a rare eastern wind, clearing out the dread and shame. Maybe, like the later-day bronze hogs outside the Spam Museum, even the Hormel pigs smiled as they were prodded to slaughter.

Family stories, and at least inferred in one letter written by him, claim that my grandfather was at that meeting in Chicago, and that his presence assured the bankers, whom he also knew personally, that the company could pull off its mandate—that A.L.'s sales machine would deliver enough revenue to get the Hormel company out of debt to the bankers. I don't know if this is true. But even if he wasn't there physically, as George Hormel suggests by focusing the meeting on himself and Jay, A.L.'s reputation remained, on that day, sound with these men. The bankers all knew him and what he'd been capable of.

Much later, George Hormel would call the Cy Thomson debacle *a blessing in disguise*. It had produced for him an epiphany: the company had *gone soft*.

This seems like the kind of epiphany a pinch-eyed man like George Hormel could only see after nearly $1.2 million had been teased out of him. In any event, his mission was now clear. The bankers had saved his company. He'd go back to work, but while he returned to Austin victorious, he was no longer in charge.

In addition to appeasing his own board of directors, George had to appeal to the creditor committee for every expenditure. Committee members may have understood banking, but none had ever run a packinghouse. The Hormel company needed to pay back its loans—totaling $4 million— as fast as it could to get the creditor committee off its back. Then the company could be George's again. Maybe then the town, and everyone in it, would forget Cy Thomson.

That would not be the case. Even seventy-five years after the embezzlement was first discovered, on my first trip to Austin, all I had to do was mention it, or the year 1921, to learn that no one had forgotten about Cy Thomson.

19.

Debits and Credits

Austin

1921–1922

No happy homecoming from the Chicago bankers committee meeting greeted A.L. Eberhart. He drove to the factory every morning, as he had for twenty years, to lead his sales team in eking out even greater value from each Hormel product and the fine grid of rail routes he knew like his middle name. A.L. had once written to a meat broker friend, *In my opinion the greatest deficiency in the management of both small and large plants today is salesmanship. I can think of very few with sales leadership in their organization. Too much volume without profit. We have succeeded here by getting new ideas into our selling.* Now, he would push to help right the House of Hormel. But first he had to explain to his colleagues in the industry what had just happened, as none of them seemed to have heard anything directly from George Hormel. So far, they'd been getting all their news from their local newspapers.

On July 22, my grandfather wrote to P.G. Gray of P.G. Gray & Co., Commission Merchants Beef and Pork Products, on State Street, in Boston:

The Butcher, the Embezzler, and the Fall Guy

The Associated Press reports as of today are approximately correct. $1,187,000.00 is the amount of R.J. Thomson's defalcation. Our accounts have regularly been audited each year by certified public accountants, Ernst & Ernst and others, and we have always been given a clean bill. This stealing has been going on in a small way since 1916, but it became very heavy in the last few months, and especially since our last annual inventory, Oct. 31, 1920. Personally my fortune is in the common stock of this company, and therefore I am flat broke, except that I have very excellent health, I never lose my nerve, I have a fair amount of ability, considerable amount of energy, and some experience that can't be taken from me, and therefore, even though I am heartily involved [in this mess] financially, as I was a large borrower using as collateral my common stock of this company, nevertheless, if I live and am given an opportunity, my debts will be liquidated dollar for dollar. I am not writing for sympathy because I know that such good loyal friends already sympathize, but I write so that you may have it firsthand. Thanks to the excellent physical condition of the firm and the excellent standing of Mr. Hormel and his associates, our high class of product manufactured, and the excellent reputation the firm has in every market they do business in, the creditor banks were indeed very broad-minded in formulating their plans with us in Chicago yesterday for the continuity of this business without its being hampered or interrupted. Everything the defaulter had is in the hands of a trustee, and he is behind bars. It is questionable what can be liquidated. His assets consist principally of three farms, all put over on a very large and elaborate scale, one having the largest flock of White Leghorn chickens in America, and another a fancy livestock breeding farm.

The emotions evoked in this letter became embedded in the stories my father told—especially that there was nothing wrong with the Hormel product, or with A.L.'s sales approach. Cy's embezzlement was the problem. A.L. would continue his winning approaches.

But even as the Hormel men got their reprieve, A.L. was facing a personal financial juggernaut. With his own loans to bankers due and overdue, with his Hormel stock having been used as collateral for those loans now worth next to nothing, with his high cost of living and his lack of cash availability post-embezzlement, my grandfather was in financial straits.

A.L. immediately took control of what he could, letting go his and Lena's household help, Elsie Procapek and Margaret Kubicek, knowing full well the effect this would have on these women whom he and Lena cared for deeply. He slimmed his ranch team at Whispering Pines. He put his two boys to work in the factory. At this moment, did he question his great gamble on Austin, Minnesota, and Geo. A. Hormel & Company? I think A.L. was too pragmatic for such introspection, at least then, and besides, introspection was better possible when out in the wilds of northern Minnesota. He simply faced each day doing whatever he could to help save the company and his family.

And there was a far greater crisis emerging on my grandfather's home front. During the awful summer of 1921 when Thomson was marshaled off to prison, Lena took ill, a sickness, like the embezzlement, that had seemed to come from nowhere. A.L.'s days and nights were a blur of Hormel work, medical consultations, and correspondence with bankers and colleagues while he strained every financial string to its breaking point, trying to find air, just as Lena tried to find hers. None of A.L.'s troubles compared with the stress of watching Lena's initial decline. Diagnosed with pleurisy, as summer turned to early fall, she didn't kick the infection.

R.C. LILLY—PRESIDENT OF MERCHANTS NATIONAL Bank in St. Paul, to which A.L. owed money—was made chair of the Hormel company creditor committee and made my grandfather's life miserable.

A.L.'s first chore was to provide an accurate accounting of his assets and liabilities. In calculating the net worth of A.L.'s stock, the accounting firms had noted that its value pre-embezzlement was $299,000. But A.L. owed $90,000 to the company, a loan taken against that stock. It was because of this financial entanglement with the company, at least in part, that the creditor committee had full right to be pressing A.L. through this period.

Through my grandfather's letters with R.C. Lilly, I was able to generate a semblance of his balance sheet in the summer of 1921. *I own my property*, my grandfather wrote to Lilly, *an undivided forty acres in the City of Austin, estimated at $100,000 in value*. But that value was his personal estimate, and it reflected the property's likely worth prior to the embezzlement, not after. Along with the plummeting Hormel stock value, the real estate market around Austin had tumbled. A.L. acknowledged in his letter to Lilly that *because no one here could afford so expensive a place, perhaps it could be liquidated for only $25,000*. Between the deflated value of his estate and the $209,000 net stock value he owned now being worth nothing, his wealth was in free fall. And it only got worse. In piecing together my grandfather's assets and liabilities, I found that he carried a lot of debt. He'd been borrowing against his stock portfolio for years to finance his investments in his home, his property at Whispering Pines, and his budding Minnesota Holstein Company. Still, pre-embezzlement, his assets were double his debts, which was plenty good enough for his lifestyle. Post-embezzlement, that was no longer the case. His debts exceeded his assets.

A.L. faced three immediate financial problems. First was his sudden lack of liquidity. His correspondence with friends clearly stated how strapped for cash he felt. The family's near-term expenses for their home, the cost of Lena's medical care, and his livestock business expenses were a knotted mess that would be tough to unwind. One thing, however, was clear: he would not sacrifice Lena's care, which at that time was entirely financed by him since the company wouldn't provide any medical benefits until much later, and there was no public medical insurance.

Second were the bankers—from Austin to Minneapolis, Chicago to Boston—who were calling in A.L.'s loans, since the collateral he'd backed them with was no longer worth anything. Through the summer and early fall, these bankers were unfriendly, unyielding, and uncompromising.

Third was his Hormel stock. A.L. had relied on that stock, nearly as cash in hand, for the prior decade, as it multiplied in certificates and value steadily every year, and he'd likely expected it to continue growing in the future. While the company was given two years to right its ship and bring its stock back to its previous value, A.L. was offered no such extensions on his loans.

These three financial strands were like twisted rope, strangling A.L.'s liquidity, his financial relationships, and his substantial pre-embezzlement wealth. They seemed intractable and he needed to deal with each in turn, while also collectively.

A.L.'s approach to his problems differed from George Hormel's. George had faced the existential threat of losing his company by leaning into his stories of the past, perhaps his own mythologizing about the company's humble beginnings and the details of building his brand. A.L., conversely, leaned into his rich and deep relationships with a strong bench of loyal friends, ones he'd cultivated and enjoyed for years.

He'd need $25,000 (over $400,000 today) in cash to get through the next quarter. Through late summer and early fall, he wrote dozens of letters to associates in multiple industries for help. Many responded as P.G. Gray did: *We have just received your letter and are about knocked stiff over your misfortune. Thomson hit you hard, old man, and no punishment is too severe for him. We know your spirit will bridge you over the ordeal.*

A.L. treasured his friends' support but needed their cash. In the ensuing weeks, five quickly came to his aid to cover his immediate needs. C.W. Riley, a provisions broker in Cincinnati, was first to respond, sending a check for $15,000 (around $248,000 today). Charlie wrote, *Presume you're still "bucking the line" and I feel certain that you will win out. Believe me, I remain your friend at all times.*

The help was appreciated, even if A.L. knew he'd need a larger amount—$75,000—the following quarter. To each of his friends he supplied a promissory note affirming that they could depend on being paid back in full in two years, mimicking the Hormel company's timeline.

A.L. had long prided himself on owning his home free and clear. Now he had to consider whether he could obtain a mortgage on it to free up cash. Swallowing his pride, he made inquiries with his bankers, but none in Minnesota would touch additional debt from associates of the Hormel company.

J.L. Mitchel, president of Austin National Bank, wrote to my grandfather of the shame he and his bank felt about the embezzlement. *You do not appreciate the extent of the embarrassment suffered by bankers holding paper either primarily made or endorsed by affiliates of George A. Hormel and Co., even though the paper may be liberally supported by stock of the Company as collateral. And you are not a depositor of this bank. We believe in and have a high personal regard for you, but the situation has tied our hands and we cannot consider an additional loan.*

This was the only letter I read from a banker that admitted their own indignity.

A.L.'s friends were uncomfortable with him trying to mortgage his home. They warned that even if he could secure one, if he was unable to make his payments on time, his family could be put out. This was unthinkable while Lena was ill.

Still, A.L. tried. He wrote to friends in Texas and Chicago to see if they might know a banker who would consider a mortgage, or if any of them personally would. These were friends who'd provided private mortgages to others in the past. In the coming weeks he received pledges for about $30,000 of the $60,000 he hoped to raise, but they remained pledges and were never consummated as loans, as far as I've been able to tell.

Many of A.L.'s letters to his colleagues were marked *personal and confidential*, which caught my eye. Some, though it appears not all, of these colleagues did business with the Hormel company. My grandfather was blurring what we'd now consider a clear boundary between a business colleague and personal friendship—and he knew he was violating that boundary, or he wouldn't have felt the need to mark his letters that way. But he'd been partnering with these men for years with the mutual goal of advancing their respective businesses. Their casual lending system had seemed to operate as a quasi-private, and privileged, banking system—as if they were all in the same family. They saw themselves as vital instruments in building our early industrial infrastructure. A.L. would surely have reciprocated with his colleagues had the tables been turned. He likely already had.

I doubt he felt he had a choice. He needed to survive. As Lena's illness worsened, and its cost mounted, A.L. did everything he could to protect her care.

Threaded through A.L.'s letters with colleagues across the country was a growing concern about the national economy. None of them felt as flush with cash in 1921 as they once had. Each held expanded debt. Their banks were growing tighter and tighter with money. The whole US economy seemed to be worsening, based on claims from his far-flung colleagues. Without cash, it was impossible to get a banking loan anywhere. W.M. Foster, of Early-Foster Commission Merchants in Waco, Texas, a cotton broker, wrote, *It would be impossible [for you] to do anything in this section of the country either. Everybody is overloaded and the banks have nothing on hand. This country is absolutely barren of money. Cotton has got to move because we carried over a good portion of last year's crop and need to get paid for it. If anything breaks I am going to send it to you because if there is one man I love from the bottom of my heart, it is you. It is just humiliating to me not to be able to send you assistance.*

In 1921, A.L. and his business associates were eight years from the stock market crash of 1929, with the Great Depression looming around that corner, and some have written that midwesterners were among the first to notice.

AS INFORMATION ABOUT CY'S EMBEZZLEMENT captivated those in Austin, it became clear that he'd perfected the art of check kiting, continuously moving Geo. A. Hormel & Company funds between banks and between states, keeping these funds in perpetual float through at least five years. Tim Corey tried to liquidate Cy's assets but brought in only about $70,000 toward the full defalcation. Animals that Cy had said were valuable proved to be sickly. Buildings he claimed to be in perfect condition were not. The facade was crumbling fast.

Rumors flew that he must have hidden his money somewhere, since it hadn't materialized in hard assets by Corey's efforts. To protect against that possibility, the Hormel company's judgment against Cy was made for $2.5 million—to cover both what had clearly been embezzled and any potential appreciation, should more money surface later, even from underground. It was the largest judgment ever issued in Mower County at the time.

Meanwhile, through the brutal second half of 1921, A.L. kept his long-term friend George Swift apprised of every move—both his own and the company's. By then, Swift had moved from Chicago to Boston, where he lived in a stately home on Commonwealth Avenue, replete with a doorman and servants and fine European paintings on its walls. The two men passed daily—sometimes twice-daily—letters between Austin and Boston and frequently resorted to telegram. Next to Lena, Swift had long been A.L.'s primary confidant and would become his closest ally as A.L. reckoned with both financial and family matters.

As winter threatened, A.L. was consumed by Lena's illness. On November 7, he wrote to Swift, *I have a lot of anxiety and worry over the financial affairs, but I now have a much greater problem to face. It is the only time in my life when I have gotten right up against a stone wall, as the highest medical authorities, namely Mayos in Rochester and Taylor in St. Paul, say Mrs. Eberhart's case is one of weeks or months.* To Foster in Waco, he wrote, *Mrs. Eberhart is confined to her bed now for several months and I've had to consult one of the best diagnosticians on the chest at over $100 and he verifies the sad information from the Mayos.*

By November, A.L. confided to Swift that working alongside his boss was growing difficult. If George Hormel had been a tough and brusque overseer, now he'd turned ornery. He was blustery with salesmen and vendors alike, affecting A.L.'s relationships with his accounts and his ability to leverage sales. *As you must know*, he wrote to Swift, *the tension has been pretty great here.*

Two weeks later and for the first time, he divulged to Swift that Lena had cancer. *She has a very rapidly growing tumor in the right lung, and there has never been a case cured. I can fight pretty hard, but running up against a stone wall like this has well near paralyzed me. I have not told her, although my two boys know, but not Elizabeth who is only twelve. I have told two or three close friends and am telling you. She is so hopeful and feels she is going to get well. I feel like a criminal every time I encourage her. But I must not only keep my own spirit up but that of the family. This is so much worse than the financial trouble.*

A.L. limped through the fall. He and George Swift strategized about how to get relief from the banks, but every proposal they sent to R.C. Lilly was met with cold regard. The National Bank of Chicago and Shawmut Bank in Boston, especially, balked, stalled, held out for more, then stalled again.

Finally, Swift and A.L. proposed a tactic they hoped would be accepted. A.L. would provide the cash he'd received from his friends to each bank in proportion to his indebtedness. In exchange, the banks would collectively release half his shares of Hormel stock. A.L. would then distribute those shares in proportion to his friends, each of whom assumed—as A.L. and George Hormel did—that the company's stock would return to its pre-embezzlement value within a few years. To sweeten the deal, George Swift would guarantee half of all of A.L.'s indebtedness to each bank, a combined $90,000 (about $1.5 million today).

The banks in Austin readily agreed. George Swift's guarantee was as good as gold, perhaps backed by bricks. On receiving this proposal, N.F. Banfield, president of First National Bank of Austin and a personal friend of the Eberhart family, wrote: *I cannot refrain from adding to this acknowledgement that this [guarantee] is evidence of a very strong friendship with Mr. Swift and is one of the most valuable things we see sometimes as we pass along this hurried, busy life of ours, something akin to David and Jonathan. I congratulate you upon having such friends.*

My grandfather had long been rich with friends. He summarized his frustration with the bigger banks in Chicago and Boston in a letter to Charlie Riley: *I never realized how hard these banks could bear down on a fellow when they thought they had him going. They weren't satisfied with the stock collateral but wanted me to deed my home to them too. And if I failed to pay on the loan within ten days' notice, they could turn me out entirely. I think by keeping my temper and diplomacy we out-generaled them because I met them with an entirely different proposition and paid them with the cash you and others loaned me on condition they release one-half my common stock collateral at each bank to turn over to my friends.*

My grandfather continued.

Not a harsh word was spoken. Cash was the weapon that seemed to satisfy the bankers' greed, A.L. continued. But even that worry, Charlie, is not half the worry of my wife's condition. She is in really bad shape, cannot get a full breath, and is in pain all the time.

In a second letter to Riley that day, A.L. wrote, *My entire value in the company was swept away overnight, but I will make that back and more. I am not allowing R.C. Lilly and the creditor committee to drive me to drink or desperation.*

ADDING TO THE PALL OVER THE EBERHART FAMILY that year was the death of A.L.'s father, Jeremiah, on August 15 at the age of eighty-five. His passing left A.L.'s mother, Emma, financially, physically, and emotionally dependent on A.L at a time when Lena could do little to help.

That month, my grandfather made the wrenching decision to hold my father back from his freshman year at the University of Minnesota. His role as second son would be to coordinate doctor and nurse visits for Lena, tend to the daily needs of his grandmother, oversee Burr Oaks, do the chores that hired men had done previously, and cheer up his younger sister. A.L. likely didn't choose his older son, Dryden, because Dryden had already started college and because my father was especially close to his mother.

A.L.'s financial problems would take years to unravel. The embezzlement ruined him by devastating his Hormel stock. The crippling cost of Lena's medical care, his lack of liquidity, the bankers' forceful pressure, and the worsening national economy were my grandfather's perfect storm and dashed his Austin dreams as they came crashing to a halt.

IT WAS AT THIS LOW POINT THAT A.L. WAS SUMMONED to his boss's office on January 22, 1922, and forced to resign. As he walked outside to his Cadillac Suburban, the frigid, dry air made it hard to breathe. His chest tightened and his lungs burned. At home, Lena lay dying.

That evening, A.L. managed to write a letter to George Swift:

> *You will probably be as much surprised as I was to know that I have resigned my position. My resignation was requested by Mr. Hormel on what seemed to me to be a very flimsy pretext. He asked me if I had personally borrowed any money of any of our brokers and I said yes. He said did you think that does the business any good, and I said I can't see that it did it any harm. He affirmed he would have to request my resignation. He mentioned that I had a breeding farm*

and that he had told me before that he did not want anyone in the business to have any outside interests. I was dumbfounded. I did not offer any argument as he is so high-strung and nervous and argument would do no good.

I believe George Hormel rid A.L. from his company for four reasons:

My grandfather had borrowed money from friends, including some of the company's brokers, and his "outside interests" in livestock investing, George believed, had distracted A.L.'s attention from Hormel concerns.

Like many CEOs feel they must, George needed to save face. In the eyes of his bankers and some of the public, he'd been blindsided by a heinous embezzlement carried out under his nose for at least eight years. He had to prove he was still in control. He needed a fall guy. He wasn't going to pick his son.

I understand these two reasons.

But I also believe that A.L.'s boss had to have been incensed by my grandfather's friendship with George Swift. For A.L. to be so close to the heir of Hormel's greatest competitor must have felt like a stick in the eye.

Finally, and most disturbing to A.L., was that George didn't fire him outright but forced him to resign. An arcane Hormel corporate bylaw required anyone who resigned from the company, for whatever reason, to offer back his stock at its current market value. There was no serious market value for Hormel stock in the aftermath of the embezzlement, which meant that Geo. A. Hormel & Company could regain two thousand shares of common stock for, essentially, nothing. To my father, this was the cheapest of George Hormel's blows as it stripped A.L. of the wealth he'd rightfully earned, and his pride in earning it. It was a cheap, if convenient, play. Far better for A.L. would have been for him to be fired outright.

I think of what Knowles Dougherty told me—that George Hormel cared first and most for his company's success. I think of what Ella Marie Lausen said—that what mattered to George most was his money. This had to be the moment when A.L. lost not only his wealth but also his faith in, and friendship with, George Hormel.

A.L. continued his letter to George Swift:

This may be a signal of the action of Lilly, as his cronies are in entire control. . . . However, I would not put it beyond [George] Hormel or Jay [Hormel] for reasons I can't write but will tell you personally when I see you. This whole deal might be a scheme to freeze me out and force me to cash in at the present depressed book value of the stock since the defalcation.

The two men traded dozens of letters on this matter. Did the wording of the bylaw signify an employee *would* turn in his stock, or that he merely *could* offer it for sale? My grandfather couldn't seek legal counsel from his close friend Samuel Catherwood, because Catherwood was the company's counsel, but legal interpretations were sought from attorneys in Boston and Chicago and appeared inconclusive. A.L. informed Swift that in no prior time when an employee had resigned the company had he been forced to give up his stock. Then again, in none of those times had the stock been so cheap to buy back.

George wrote in his unpublished autobiography that his decision to ask for my grandfather's resignation was *the most difficult decision* he ever made, but that he felt his executives had gone soft after World War I when selling was easy, and that my grandfather had lost his drive for performance. It's true that complacency is a danger in any high-performing company, something I've seen play out in several, and have advised CEOs to guard against. But it's also remediable with effective leadership. George didn't have those kinds of skills.

Maybe the company's 1980s CEO, Richard Knowlton, had been right to tell Knowles that the company owed us an apology. Maybe it did.

20.

If There's Anything in Prayer, I Certainly Ought to Get Well

Austin

1921–1922

One afternoon in the middle of July 1921, A.L. returned home at midday, as was usual, to assist in Lena's care and to soothe her discomfort. Lena was especially short of breath that afternoon, her dark hair matted against her damp brow. She complained of pain in her shoulder but also rubbed her chest where it hurt most.

A.L. tried to distract her with stories from their early married life in St. Paul. This had sometimes worked. They'd reminisce quietly about a time when all ahead looked fresh and ripe with opportunity—just the two of them in the full of their attraction, setting up their first home, taking on the world together. A.L. wanted Lena to smile again, to remind him of the girl he'd chosen to spend the rest of his life with. That day their intimacies brought laughter, but with that, greater pain.

"Oh," Lena said. "I wish I could do it without it hurting."

From then forward, A.L. worked hard to ensure that Austin friends and Lena's family visited regularly, and when he was home, he encouraged my father to get outside for a hike, or later that winter, to skate on the frozen-over river.

"You must get out when you can," A.L. told him.

Between the discovery of the embezzlement in July 1921 and my grandfather's resignation in January 1922, Lena was visited frequently by doctors and nurses who injected her with morphine for pain and prescribed slugs of whiskey, or fistfuls of pills. Nothing seemed to make any difference in her condition, which was only worsening.

Lillian Hormel was a frequent visitor of Lena's and would continue until Lena's death. She often helped with household chores like mending and darning. Lena's best friend, Adah Crane, came each day. Lena wondered if she'd live long enough to set the ledger straight with these good friends.

Lillian and Lena's conversations must have ranged widely: about how their children were growing, their time on the Hormel board, raising money from Andrew Carnegie for the public library, hosting the well-child clinic and Duo meetings, and the annual company picnics. Along with greased pig and pie-eating contests, the picnics had been highlights of both women's pasts. That summer there would be none; every person employed by Hormel was focused on saving the company.

A group of Christian Scientists had formed a community in Austin, and Lillian Hormel read to Lena from the teachings of its founder, Mary Baker Eddy. (This is described in my father's journal and in stories from cousins, but I've found no other record of Lillian Hormel's interest in Christian Science.) These visits, in addition to Lena's debilitating illness, raised doubts in her own faith.

"If your faith is strong enough," Lillian would tell her, "God will save you."

But no amount of praying or faith expression had cured Lena yet, even though her diagnosis in the early part of the second half of 1921 had been pleurisy, something one could recover from.

While she wanted to believe, Lena's doubt persisted. As she confided to my father, "It's easy for Lillian to say when she hasn't been sick a day in her life. But then maybe that's just the weakness in me speaking."

AFTER THE HORMEL MEN BROKERED A REPRIEVE for the company, Dryden left for his second year at the University of Minnesota while my father harvested apples from the orchard, chopped wood for the winter, fed fires as the nights grew cold, and emptied fireplace ashes on the outside gardens. He fixed broken windows and cranked Sunday ice cream. He sorted daily correspondence and answered what letters he could.

When his mother needed medical observation or an injection for pain, he called for a nurse or doctor. He lifted his sister Elizabeth's spirit by driving her and her friends to picture shows.

Lena had been my father's earliest poetic champion. And his father needed him. Still, his friends had gone off to college, along with his older brother, and he was on his own every day with a mother whose health was failing. Dryden wrote to him from Minneapolis on October 16: *I hope you are able to live though the loneliness of your job and loss of friends and*

hope that Mother improves. Give her my love and the best of your attention.

I never heard my father say that he resented this period. Later he'd say it fueled his poetry. But as I read through his journal from that year, I was surprised by how much was expected of him at the age of seventeen. It would have been a lot for anyone to bear.

Some manner of routine was established at Burr Oaks by late fall, while bankers and creditors pressed A.L. for money and his friends rallied in support of both his financial and emotional needs. B.J. Mumm of F.J. Mumm Company in St. Paul wrote, *One thing, A.L., that I would say is not to give up about Lena's health.*

The specter of Thanksgiving, helmed by my father and not Lena, pained the Eberhart children. Outside, the Cedar River was frozen over, but there would be little time for skating and no ice fishing that winter. My father carried Lena to the upstairs hallway, where a window seat looked out on the beauty of the frozen river separating the Eberhart home from the Hormel company on the other side. Elizabeth brought her dolls and played quietly next to her mother while Lena dozed in this warm retreat.

My grandmother woke on Thanksgiving morning in fearful anguish. My father called for the doctor, and Lena told him she didn't know how much more pain she could abide. She felt her family's love and warmth around her, but nothing—prayer, love, pills, whiskey, morphine—had reduced her agony. A.L. and his boys knew she had cancer, though he'd not yet spoken of it to his daughter, nor to Lena. By today's standards this seems like a grave injustice to my grandmother, but back then women were often "protected" from such information.

My father carried the holiday turkey upstairs for Lena to witness. With a bowl of stuffing at her bedside, he handed his mother the spices so she could assist with the preparations. She breathed in as best she could the sweet aromas of dried onion and clove and brightened briefly at seeing the large bird.

"There, Dick," she said as she spooned in the aromatics. "Now it will be just right."

It was a busy morning at Burr Oaks, and Lena's spirits lifted sufficiently for her to dress herself in her finest black organza gown, its bodice covered in chiffon.

"You look lovely," my father said as he carried her down to the dining room, where she joined the family in giving thanks. In photographs from that day, likely taken after the meal, Lena wears a string of pearls around her neck and is seated in a wicker chair in the living room by the large windows full of flowering plants. Her long hair is twisted into a bun at the back of her head, loose curls outlining her face.

After the holiday meal, A.L. returned to the factory—never suspecting that his dismissal from the company was only two months away—and my father returned Lena to her room. That afternoon, she called her three children to her side and made out her personal will.

"You must be strong," she said as she gave her diamond pin to Elizabeth and her leather-bound Shakespeare set to my father. She also gave her pearl engagement ring to Dad and another ring to Dryden, reasoning the boys would marry one day and could use them for their engagements. Surely she knew she had little time left, if not the name of her disease.

AT THE COMPANY, THE UNIVERSITY OF NEBRASKA standout Tim Corey was doing his best to liquidate the assets of Ransome J. Thomson, and Samuel Catherwood was trying to convince George Hormel to sue Ernst & Ernst and the Austin banks through which the embezzled money had been funneled to

Oak Dale Farms. Catherwood argued that such a suit might garner back most of the stolen money. George considered the proposal but turned it down. It would ruin Ernst & Ernst, he reasoned, at a time when the best accounting firm was just establishing itself. And it would damage the banks. A legal suit would be a distraction; *a year's investment in the business, however,* he wrote, *might go a long way toward paying off the lost money, and produce results for years to come, while harming no one.*

I've heard similar choices debated in C-suites and as a bank director. Litigation is expensive and time-consuming, and its success uncertain. George was right that it could have been enormously distracting. He wanted all energy focused on earning back through sales the money taken and ensuring the value of a share of Hormel stock would, in two years time, be worth at least what it had been. He, and my grandfather, had confidence the company would accomplish this feat.

THE DAY AFTER THANKSGIVING, LENA TURNED forty-eight. Nearly one hundred birthday cards swamped the entry at Burr Oaks, along with dozens of boxes of fresh flowers. *It looked like a bower,* my father wrote in his journal.

Seems too bad I can't get well, Lena confided to Dad. *Elizabeth needs me. If there's anything in prayer, I certainly ought to get well.*

The day after her birthday, A.L. took one of several trips to consult with Will and Charlie Mayo, two physicians in Rochester who had recently built their "clinic in a cornfield." The Mayos believed Lena should receive daily X-ray treatments. A.L. purchased a machine and installed it in the gymnasium, there being no X-ray equipment closer than forty miles away. Each day, he or my father carried Lena down two flights for treatment, though they appear to have done little but increase Lena's nausea and vomiting. Lena felt she had suffered enough and conversed about this with A.L., my father, Lillian Hormel, and Adah Crane. Still, she didn't want to give up whatever time she had left.

Later that month, A.L. learned of a new procedure with a Chicago lung specialist that had been invented in Germany where three women in her condition had recovered. He got on a train to Chicago for consultation, but, three days later, returned home with sobering news. Lena might recover if she underwent the treatment, but if it didn't cure her, it could kill her. My dad's journal entry says the 80,000 volts of radiation would be administered over a single six-hour period, such being the state of advanced cancer care in 1921.

My father found it hard to believe his mother didn't know she had cancer. When I described Lena's symptoms to my own physician, he speculated that her lung cancer might have started in her breast, because she described such pain in her shoulder. Back then, a woman might not have talked about discomfort in her breast, and it is possible a diagnosis and treatment would have been delayed until the cancer had metastasized to her lung, at which point it was probably too late.

On A.L.'s return from Chicago, the family spent a week considering the possible treatment. Lena then knew she had a tumor, and she confided to Adah and my father that she thought the treatment was her last chance. Then she called for the family doctor and asked for his advice.

"If your wife was in my state, would you have her go?" she asked him.

"I would," the doctor said, his face forlorn.

In the end, Lena made the decision to go as she'd made all her most important decisions in life—with careful thought and reflection and buoyed by the love of her family and friends—and for this one, a strong will to survive. Her sons were men then—sixteen and eighteen—but Elizabeth was only twelve. For her, primarily, Lena would go.

ON DECEMBER 18, TWO WEEKS AFTER LENA'S birthday, the children ventured out to the far end of Burr Oaks in a snowfall and cut a small, early Christmas tree. After hauling the tree upstairs to Lena's room, they topped it with a star, clipped candle holders to its arching branches, and lit candles. They gathered small gifts beneath the tree while A.L. soothed his family with Christmas carols from the piano downstairs.

"You must pray for my return," Lena told her children that night.

A.L. later corresponded with a friend about what Lena had told him that evening: *If anything happens to me*, she had said, *you must be sure Dick goes to college next year. And Adah and Ralph Crane will care for Elizabeth. A daughter will always need a mother.*

ON THE DAY OF DEPARTURE, MY FATHER HELPED a frail Lena into her heavy wool coat and guided her out to the ambulance. A.L. and Lena boarded the train and settled into a stateroom. As their train pulled out of Austin, they watched their tearful children on the platform, snowflakes falling on their cheeks. Adah and Ralph Crane steadied them, saying they'd go to the high school basketball game that evening, a hopeful distraction. (Thankfully, Austin High School beat Albert Lea that night, 70–62.)

The following day, the children received a telegram from their father in Chicago. Lena's frail state could not endure the rigor of such extensive radiation treatments. The doctor planned for several smaller treatments over three days, but it would still be a grueling procedure.

Ten days later, Lena was strong enough to return home to Austin, but the treatments did little good.

ON JANUARY 15, 1922, ONE WEEK BEFORE A.L. was forced to resign, Doak Catherwood came by Burr Oaks to see his friend. They smoked cigars and drank brandy while my father assisted his mother and grandmother. Was Catherwood merely visiting his good friend in a time of need? Might he have been confidentially warning him of an impending change in employment? In the letter my father wrote to Dryden that day, he didn't convey what his father and Catherwood talked about, but in A.L.'s letter to George Swift on the evening of his forced resignation, he noted:

> *I asked [George Hormel] if the resignation was demanded by the creditor committee or if it was on his own initiative, and he said he did not consider it necessary to tell me. I handed in my resignations as officer and director in the three corporations—the Austin plant, the mill, and the Texas company—and they were accepted as of Feb. 1st, but he agreed, when I asked, to continue my salary for six months without working. I really can't write more details but when I see you will tell you some interesting things.*

I wish I knew what those *interesting things* were.

In all his correspondence with friends, A.L. laid out the facts as he saw them, not asking for sympathy but telling the truth. Whatever speculations he may have had about his firing, the Hormel company worked hard to choreograph and control the narrative of such a high-profile dismissal to protect its reputation. A.L.'s resignation was blamed in large part on Lena's illness. This was a blow to read. A.L.

had worked more than full-time during his wife's illness without complaint—even during his trip to Chicago for the consultation with the specialist he had conducted Hormel business there. It's inconceivable he ever seriously considered resigning of his own accord.

On February 15, *The Squeal*, Hormel's internal newsletter, published a whitewashed version of A.L.'s fall from grace.

A.L. Eberhart Resigns. *It is with sincere regret that we announce the resignation of A.L. Eberhart, Vice President, which took effect February 1st. On account of Mrs. Eberhart's serious illness, Mr. Eberhart considered* *it advisable to give up all duties pending her complete recovery. When Mr. Eberhart first came to the company in 1900, the business was relatively small; only 23,355 hogs were killed during the entire year. There have been many single weeks during the past year when the number of hogs killed was materially greater than the yearly total of 1900. . . It was his sales genius that conceived the mixed [rail] car idea and his sales ability that put it across. Shortly after the war . . . Mr. Eberhart was instrumental in getting eleven of the principal packers together to organize the American Provisions Export Company, which has become one of the largest factors in the [country's] export meat business. He was also one of "APEC's" committee of three that went abroad to place agencies in the principal European countries. Although he never aspired to be President of APEC, he was recognized as one of its leading spirits. His enthusiasm, magnetic personality, and methods of square dealing have made him one of the best-known packinghouse men in the country and won for him more warm friends than it is the good fortune of most men to possess. There are a great many people in the organization both in the office and on the road who owe a great deal to Mr. Eberhart for his helpful suggestions and splendid sales ideas. When he talks he radiates energy and optimism. He has the rare faculty of being able to instill in the minds of his listeners the idea "He who admits not defeat is seldom defeated." Mr. Eberhart has made no plans, but those of us who have worked with him know that it will be a fortunate organization that attracts to itself his energy, wisdom, and proven ability.*

Just as CEOs hope their companies are too big to fail, some believe the same of themselves. My grandfather learned otherwise. By March, as A.L. and George Swift traded letters and strategized about corporate bylaws and the continuing costs for Lena's medical care, A.L. saw no option but to seek new employment. I do not know if this negated his Hormel salary, or if George Hormel, as his friend, ever discouraged him from taking the job at a time when his wife was dying, but A.L. was picked up quickly for an executive position with Dold Packing Company in Omaha, Nebraska. The job required him to live there—300 miles from Austin—only returning home to Lena on weekends.

Lena was now in unremitting pain, dampened only by morphine. Each weekend, he and Lena commiserated over whether each day might be their last together. He telegrammed his family every day from Omaha, and each night he penned four brief letters: one to his wife and one to each of his three children. On May 23, he wrote to Lena,

> *I was indeed happy this morning to know that you had a better day yesterday. I believe with letting up on the inoculations that you will soon show a better condition. I surely hope so. Pardon the haste but I wanted you to get this tomorrow morning and to know that I think of you always and only wish that I could stand this suffering myself instead of you.*

My father carried Lena downstairs for the last time in early June. She gave her wedding ring back to A.L., assuming he would have a chance to remarry.

On the night of June 22, my father filled his mother's room with pussy willows. After falling asleep on the daybed in Lena's room, he woke around 9:30 p.m. in what he referred to in his journal as a *luminous stillness*. He helped his mother take a sip of water through a glass straw. The nurse told him to go for the doctor.

My father gunned the Cadillac Suburban to Lafayette Park, where the doctor was attending the annual Chautauqua. When they returned to Lena's room, all was still.

Lena's last breath came on her twenty-fourth wedding anniversary. She was just forty-eight years old.

The *Austin Daily Herald* wrote of my grandmother:

In the death of Mrs. Eberhart, Austin has lost a loved and lovely woman. Few characters exemplified more vividly the beauty of womanhood than she. All classes united in sorrow for her suffering and in regret that a life so useful and wholesome had so soon to close. She was gifted with a personality that radiated kindness and good will. Her benevolent face, the softness of her voice, her cordiality and social charm were no less to be admired than the candor of her soul, which scorned deceit and never wore a mask.

The following year, A.L. brought suit against Geo. A. Hormel & Company for relief in giving up his stock. The company countersued. Eventually, in 1923, an out-of-court settlement was arranged. I wonder if Doak Catherwood helped broker that support for A.L., or if he steadfastly held to Hormel's desires. Based on family records, my grandfather received about $75,000 in cash, or 37 percent of his stock's net pre-embezzlement value. Cash was needed, but he'd never benefit from Hormel stock ownership again.

A.L. worked hard till the day he died and—with much assistance from his son Dryden—eventually paid back every debt he owed to his bankers and friends from the Austin years. While he held key positions in the meat industry throughout his life, he never again came close to obtaining the kind of wealth he'd once possessed in Austin.

21.

Poetry Slam

Austin

2000

On the final day of our public responsibilities for the poetry celebration in Austin, my brother and I head over to the public library for a more casual event, one I've been looking forward to—a poetry slam for the city's teens.

Inside the Austin Public Library, a glass wall extends the length of the north side of the building, facing Mill Pond, a man-made water body on the Cedar River. This is the successor library to the original that my grandmother and Lillian Hormel helped raise money for eighty years ago. Fading sun through a western window lights the wooden stacks holding thousands of titles, lined up in rows ahead of us. Burr Oaks was not far upriver from this spot.

Dikkon and I have become acquainted with the newly appointed high school principal, Joe Brown. Just hired in June, he exudes passion and energy for the kids in his charge. He arrives right after us, and I shake his hand with familiarity. As our palms join, I notice that he's still sporting an *Al Gore for President* pin on his sports coat.

Dikkon tours the library for a moment, then heads into the community room.

"Austin's changed since my first trip here," I say to Joe. "Am I wrong, or is it becoming more diverse?"

"You've noticed."

"Back in the early 1900s, when my grandparents lived here, it was mostly full of Scandinavians and Germans."

He nods. "Now they're from everywhere, but especially Mexico, Cuba, and Africa."

"How has that changed the schools?" I ask.

"We have thirty native languages spoken in our schools, and a need to support them," he says.

The first student shows up, and Joe greets her and introduces me. A petite girl, she's just starting her freshman year. She heads into the meeting room while we wait to greet more students.

"Do you suppose Hormel employees and their kids now are as loyal to the company as they might have been in the early 1920s?" I'm trying to get a sense of this place, and I know Joe has current information about Austin.

"I can't answer that," he says. "But families here have depended on the company for employment for a long time. It's our largest company and the Austin plant is the company's biggest plant with over a thousand employees."

"I get the sense that residents have high regard for the company."

"Like any big company, there's a yes and no answer to that. I suspect the loyalty is lower now since it's no longer run by Hormel family members. But it provides good-paying jobs and helps maintain an even economy here, though many employees work in its plants outside Austin."

I nod. "That makes sense."

I shake hands with three more students who arrive one by one.

"The company is a good citizen," Joe notes, "which everyone appreciates." He nods to a small knot of juniors as they saunter in. One especially shy boy doesn't raise his eyes from his sneakers. Joe greets each kid warmly.

"I'm looking forward to hearing what these kids have to say," I tell him.

"This weekend has sparked a new interest in poetry," he says. "Austin's had a proud tradition in the arts. Along with strong academics and competitive sports."

My eyes widen. "I'm not used to seeing four thousand students at a high school football game!"

He chuckles. "We like our football. But I've challenged the boys to attend all the girls' games too. They deserve as much recognition."

"I've been impressed with each of the schools we've been in. Such energy. And the teachers all seem great. You've clearly got a good school system." I am accustomed to observing companies, not schools, but I know positive energy and openness when I see them.

"That we do." Joe gestures toward the meeting room. "Shall we join them?"

INSIDE THE ROOM, CHAIRS ARE SET UP IN A BIG circle, and every one is full. A dozen kids have taken their seats, along with Dikkon and half a dozen English teachers. Just the right number to make the event feel important, while still intimate.

Joe opens the slam by suggesting that Dikkon and I read a few of Dad's poems. My brother chooses "The Groundhog" and "The Fury of Aerial Bombardment." I add "One Morning in Maine" and "Rumination." As our father did when he read his poems, we either pre-load or follow each one with a short story of how, where, and when it came to be.

It's time to hear from the kids.

The Butcher, the Embezzler, and the Fall Guy

First is a rhymed couplet about a snowy winter in Austin; next a sonnet about first love. We hear haikus, a rap-style lyric, a long narrative poem about a young girl's fear of pregnancy. We hear about the kids' mothers and fathers, their teachers, their friends. We hear about childhood trauma. A football player describes the anxiety he feels about his father who is serving in Iraq and whether he'll make it home. I'm astonished by the vulnerability and candor of these young authors. I could not have written anything like these poems at their age, or shared them publicly. In the late 1960s, though, there was also no such opportunity.

I'm swept up in the lives and passions of these kids while simultaneously pulled back to my parents' living room when I was a child. That room was filled with young students like these, if a few years older, and in college. At the time, they were all boys, as Dartmouth hadn't yet accepted women undergrads. I grew up surrounded by poetry, listening to voice, meter, and phrasing. Words mattered, as did stories. There is no critique here, only approval and encouragement. How many small cities in the Midwest—or anywhere—would have conceived of this three-day weekend devoted to poetry, let alone pulled it off? My affection for this place grows.

Scanning the students of this brand-new century, with their various hairstyles, their eager bodies, their chosen attire, their midwestern lilt, I think about how Austin continues to define me as I try to define it. The kids make me hopeful, and a random idea pops up: What if our family could help them keep writing poems? What if the idea that Austin has set in motion—the insistence on studying the poetic form—could be continued? What if we could see this celebration into the future?

I look over at Joe. I think he'd be in favor. And Mike Ruzek has proven he knows how to get things done. I glance at my brother and tuck away the idea for later.

22.

Visionary Farms

LeRoy, Minnesota

2000

On Saturday morning, the final day of our father's celebration in Austin, Dikkon and I meet up with Ella Marie Lausen, who has cleared her afternoon to show us what remains of Oak Dale Farms in LeRoy. I'll call the place "Visionary Farms" after my father's verse play, which portrays Cy Thomson's rise to prominence, his embezzlement from the Hormel company, and its cataclysmic effect on A.L. The play, first published in 1950, ran through multiple theatrical shows on stages in Seattle, Des Moines, and Boston.

Ella Marie is in her late seventies now, with a sharp mind and a slight tremor in her hands. She and I have corresponded regularly through the last three years, her letters in hand script on greeting cards, mine printed from my MacBook and mailed. She inserts each card inside manila envelopes stuffed with news clippings and documents she thinks will be of interest to me. I savor each package as a window into another corner of our country and my family's history. Through our correspondence, our friendship has deepened.

In her low-slung sedan, Ella Marie pegs a speed just below the highway's legal limit. I ask her again why she thinks my grandfather was forced to resign. She demurs.

"It's a puzzle to me," she says. "People were unhappy when he was fired. No one thought he had anything to do with the embezzlement. But," she adds, "I have to live here."

I take this to suggest it's impolitic to speak ill of George Hormel, and I hold off, wanting to respect that boundary.

"What I've arranged," she says to my brother and me, "is to have you meet with Merrill Chesebrough at his church for lunch, before we head to Oak Dale Farms to see what's left." She pronounces Merrill's name "Merle," as he will.

Ella Marie slows her car as we pull into LeRoy. We pass a John Deere, an Amoco, a Farmers Cooperative Creamery, three churches, and the library. A population sign, posted where prairie land leans out for the horizon in all directions, reads "904."

Ella Marie has shown me photographs of Thomson's businesses and LeRoy's main street back in 1920, with its large brick buildings, its new hotels, its proximity to the railroad station, its wide main street. Driving into town this morning, there is no such bustle. Brick has given way to wooden construction and low-slung pizza joints. It's a town of a thousand people now, with no pizazz.

We find the First Presbyterian Church, where Merrill takes his Saturday lunch alongside fellow parishioners. Except for two army stints in World War II and Korea, Merrill is a lifelong resident of LeRoy. His father, publisher of the *LeRoy Independent*, died while he was in high school. Merrill helped his mother keep up the newspaper, then took it over years later, after she passed away. It was the *LeRoy Independent* that serialized Cy Thomson's autobiography as he wrote each chapter from prison.

Eighty-one-year-old Merrill will be the first person I've

met who knew Cy personally. His parents were close friends of Cy and Maude.

We pull into the church parking lot at 12:15 p.m. Descending the steep staircase to the basement community room, we're met with a rising tide of sounds and aromas: honeyed, braised beef; yeasty sandwich buns; sweet mayonnaise on a coleslaw; the candied earthiness of baked beans. My eyes fill, as these smells evoke every church supper my mom took us to during our summers in Maine. Back then, church suppers were one of the few places we could go "out" for dinner.

Sun slants through the underground community room's clerestory windows and we look out on a small sea of white-haired elders, dressed in country cottons, enjoying a meal together.

Dikkon bounces on one foot as he leans into me. "I feel like I've walked into a novel," he says. Like my father, my brother is a romantic. He and I lower the average age in the room by two decades, and all eyes are on us until we take our seats at Merrill's table. Then, we're treated like part of his family.

My role here is to find out as much as I can. I'm excited to talk to Merrill, since he lived through the period I'm researching.

"What did you think of George Hormel?" I ask for starters.

"George A. was for George A.," Merrill says succinctly. "He wasn't friendly to you unless you were helping him make money."

I jot down what Merrill says.

"Tell me about Oak Dale Farms," I say.

"I went out there nearly every day. With my chums. On our bikes."

"How far is it from here?" I ask.

"Oh, a mile."

Merrill is a tall man whose legs extend under the table from his side to mine. I place myself at an angle so as not to crowd him. It's hard to tell he's past eighty. He's engaging and has a sharp mind. His memory is good. With his punchy, headline-like responses to my questions, he sounds like a newspaperman—someone interested in real-life stories who sticks to the facts.

Ella Marie and Merrill know each other from serving on the Mower County Fair board. She tells us about his community service—including the regional development commission and the board of the county mental health agency. He's a current director of First National Bank of LeRoy, one of the banks that did business with the Hormel company and Cy Thomson. He's served as the town's mayor and its treasurer.

"So you had fun out at the farm," I say, returning to Oak Dale, as Ella Marie, Dikkon, and I pass bowls of food and fill our plates.

"It was the best thing for miles, right in our backyard." Merrill laughs. "The hall of mirrors was . . . well, I remember that—how funny we all looked."

I think of the room of mirrors my father used to take us to at Perry's Nut House in Belfast, Maine. Looking fat, then skinny, then tall, then short. Now I'm on my bike with Merrill, on the road to Oak Dale Farms and looking at myself in the mirrors. I'm no longer reading stale newspapers. I'm there.

"Did you have to pay to get in?" I ask.

"Ten cents in a milk can by the gate," he says.

"Was that a lot back then?" Dikkon asks.

"It sure felt like it." Merrill nods. "But it was worth every penny."

"What about the children's playground?" I ask. "I've heard there were rides of a kind."

"Oh, yes, especially a roller coaster," Merrill says, his eyes lighting up, a broad smile covering his face. "I could have ridden that all day long."

"A roller coaster in LeRoy," Dikkon says. "No kidding!"

"First of its kind in the country, we heard. I know one thing about Thomson: he was quite an inventor, along with everything else." Merrill's hands move through the air as he animates his story. "He built this wide staircase—maybe a dozen feet and thirty feet high—right out in the field."

"Wait, that's like three stories," I say.

"It was near the baseball field. So at the top we could look out over the crowds. We could hear the bats hit the balls and watch runners take off from home plate. The whole contraption was covered with this dark green rubber, and motorized."

"No kidding," Dikkon repeats.

Merrill laughs.

"It's sounding more like an escalator to me?" I say quizzically.

"It felt like a roller coaster," Merrill replies, still grinning. "It carried you up and down, and it was high enough to be a little scary. We loved it."

"The kind of thing young boys would like," Dikkon says.

"Tell us about your parents," I say. "I've heard they were friends with Cy and Maude."

"Oh, yes," Merrill says, bobbing his head. "Fine friends. Everyone knew them. They came for supper. Always polite and nice."

He reminds me that Maude died while Cy was in prison. Merrill's mother was incensed that when Cy requested permission to attend her funeral, a judge declined. After Cy was finally released from Stillwater prison, Merrill's mother continued to socialize with him.

"So, despite the embezzlement, they remained friends," I say.

"They did. At least for a time."

Merrill looks pensive, making me think I should head us to a different question, though I do hope to circle back to this point later.

"Was there a swimming pool?" I ask.

"The largest west of Chicago."

Pride spreads across Merrill's face.

"You were pleased with his achievements," I say.

"We were."

"What about the dance hall?" I ask. "Were you ever inside?"

"Oh, my word." Merrill shakes his head. "I never saw the insides of it, but my parents went and I heard all about it. It was designed by the same architect who did the Hippodrome! Inside, it had a clear span with a shiny hardwood floor. It could handle a thousand couples. And two thousand light bulbs in that room. That itself was something! Just to have all that light. There were vaudeville shows. All the big bands came to play. Jimmy Dorsey. Lawrence Welk. Even Count Basie."

Merrill's telling the same story, the same way, that my father did. He's using the same phrases, the same intonation. It's as if everyone here has the same script and plays their amazement and horror the same way. Maybe my father wasn't exaggerating when it came to Oak Dale Farms.

Merrill says it was through the last three years of Cy's embezzling that the place took off and people just swarmed there.

"From Iowa and Minnesota, but also Texas and California and all over. And especially Chicago. They'd arrive Friday night or Saturday morning and spend the weekend with animals, watching ball games, eating barbecue."

I've heard about Oak Dale Farms from many; now I can see how it might have brought a community together after the war.

"Did George Hormel make it out there?" I ask.

"I don't know. I would think he would have. Jay Hormel certainly did. He and Cy were good friends."

This is news. It's clear everyone in the Hormel orbit was taken by Cy.

"He came more than once. The last time, I believe, he stayed at the hotel in LeRoy. I've heard he had a good-looking blonde on his arm, and when they registered for the night he sent her upstairs, saying, 'I'll be up in a minute.'"

"So, a woman other than his wife?" I ask.

Merrill nods.

This is a side of Jay I haven't heard before. I make a note of this on my pad.

"I've read that Cy sold red mailboxes to farmers to mark the Oak Dale Trail to his farms and influenced the railroads to bring their Pullmans to LeRoy," I say.

"He was a born salesman, maybe as good as your grandfather."

That's a comparison I haven't thought of.

"And he tried to get the state to help out," I say.

"He tried to get whatever he could from everyone," Merrill explains. "But government officials were too slow, so he took it upon himself."

"He wasn't called 'Cyclone' for nothing," I say.

"No. He was well known, and highly respected, right up to the governor," Merrill says. "It was part of his allure, I think—that if you knew Cy, you might get to know others."

This makes sense.

Merrill looks at me, gauging the effect of his prior words. "I hope I didn't offend you about him being like your grandfather."

"No," I say, half-truthfully. Cy Thomson and my grandfather were selling entirely different things, after all: the former, a mirage; the latter, hard sales numbers for George Hormel. Merrill speaks at such a clip I'm sure I'm missing things as I scrawl my notes.

"Cy gave us something to be proud of," he says, nearly wistful. "It was a high time. But I don't see it that way anymore."

I register the comment, then ask, "What happened to him after he got out of prison?" I haven't found much of anything about the years after he served his sentence, except that he initially came home to LeRoy.

"He served eight and a half years of his fifteen-year sentence," Merrill says.

"Then what happened?"

"He returned to LeRoy, but then moved away. After that there was little information about him." Merrill furrows his brow and looks at his plate, measuring his words. "He finished his time around 1930, I think, and then he was incarcerated a second time. I think it was in 1941."

"Really?" I ask. Why hasn't anyone told me this? Did my father know? I look at Ella Marie, and she looks as surprised as I am.

"On a morals charge," Merrill explains.

Merrill looks me in the eye but seems unsure whether to proceed. Because I'm a woman? From out of town? In his church basement?

"What do you mean by a morals charge?" I nudge.

"Something to do with young boys, is what I heard. At his arraignment he told the judge he'd learned to be homosexual in prison."

I raise my eyebrows.

Merrill folds his arms over his chest and sets his jaw. I catch a faint shake of his head, as if he can't believe this fact about Cy, or he's as skeptical about the excuse as I am. Might Cy Thomson have been a closeted gay man? *Or*, I think, horrified, *is it possible that he was a pedophile?*

"Wasn't he superintendent of the Sunday school my father attended?" I ask.

"He was," Ella Marie confirms.

I look at Merrill, then Ella Marie, then Dikkon. I'm not sure what Cy's sexual preferences have to do with my grandfather's story, but I make a note to see if I can track down the second charge. It would only matter if it turned out he was a pedophile, and if he'd used his ten-acre children's playground as a grooming ground. But wait—I've never heard anything about kids being abused at Oak Dale Farms. I rein in my speculations.

"I get the impression that even seventy-five years later, a lot of people in Austin are still fascinated by Cy Thomson."

"They are," Merrill agrees. "Here too. He was a big-hearted benefactor. It all seemed so real. We wanted it to be. It's still confounding."

So, a generous cyclone blows into town, rises to prominence at the Hormel company, and then, with no explicable reason for his excess money, creates a fantasy enterprise that raises prize-winning animals and entertains tens of thousands while providing employment opportunity that hadn't before existed. Then it collapses as fast as a dust ball whiffed across the prairie. People working at his farms—a lot of them—must have lost their jobs after he was caught. I haven't thought about them before. And all of this set in motion by a scrawny farm kid from Cresco from whom no one expected much.

"My dad focused so much on his father's firing and his loss of wealth that I hadn't understood until now how many others must have suffered," I admit.

Merrill shakes his head, still in disbelief. Ella Marie nods.

"After the morals charge," Merrill continues, "let's just say his popularity declined. People pulled away from supporting him."

"And your mother?" I ask.

"She too."

Ella Marie scoops out portions of piping-hot Brown Betty, and we cover our plates in fake whipped cream.

Digging into our Betty, I look at her and whisper, "Thank you"—not just for this comfort food but for introducing me to Merrill. Through my consulting work, I've leaned on my instinct for who and what is trustworthy. Merrill fits that bill—as does the information he's shared today.

Lunch winds down. We help pick up tables, wish parishioners well on their way, and head out to Merrill's car. He insists on driving us to Cresco to see what my father called "Visionary Farms."

IT'S A FEW-MINUTE DRIVE SOUTHEAST TO OAK DALE Farms and Amusement Park, just over the state line, in Iowa. All I see is prairie, with country-style houses and small family ranches. There aren't any Oak Dale Farms buildings left anymore.

Merrill tells me he's gained permission from the current owner of what was Cy's land for us to wander around. She greets us at her door and waves us along.

The farmland that's left, now parceled off and turned over for winter, is as brown as the darkest cocoa. The rolling lands of Iowa and Minnesota are possessed of the blackest earth, and the most enormous skies, I've ever seen. I look out and picture hundreds of sedans packed in on a weekend eight decades ago. I imagine ladies in slim-waisted dresses and brimmed hats festooned with ribbons, ushering their children to the playground as men in dark suits and stiff white shirts talk livestock prices and grouse about a lack of rain. It's a freeze-frame I'll carry home with me.

Dikkon wanders off on his own. I gesture to Merrill and Ella Marie. Merrill shows us the corner backstop for the baseball diamond, formerly surrounded by a grandstand and bleachers. I imagine young men rounding the bases, gunning for home, their baseballs sailing far in the humid Iowa air.

"I used to think Cy made all his money from the dimes we dropped in his milk cans." Merrill laughs.

"Apparently it wasn't all from those buckets!"

"There were baseball teams that came to play here," he muses. "I remember Cicero Littrell and Cy Slapnicka."

"They were big?" I ask.

"Oh yes."

I'm nostalgic for this era when you could while away a happy Saturday at a hybrid country fair/amusement park, watching young men swing their bats on a hot July day. "I wish I'd been here back then."

Merrill chokes up. "It really was something."

He pulls us over to the remaining wall of the swimming pool. What's left is pockmarked and crumbling. I'm quieted by the ghosts that I feel around me—ghosts of generosity and invention, of hubris and lies, of scandal and greed.

I scan the gunmetal sky and listen to the caw of a jet-black crow. A murder of them flies by, darkening my mood. Despite its ghosts, I feel connected to this land. To the memory of my grandparents and their dreams; to my father's poems, sprouting from shallow hillsides filled with daisies. My family's fate was sealed here on this black earth. My grandfather trusted these wild, open spaces and his friends George Hormel and Cy Thomson—never losing the gleam in his eye, never suspecting each would betray him.

MERRILL AND ELLA MARIE HEAD BACK TO the car. Dikkon, too, from a different direction.

I linger for a moment, but have what I've come for. The sights, the sounds, the feel of this place. The bigness, along with its exposed underbelly.

I close my hand around a fistful of cold, jet-black earth. This is my third trip to southern Minnesota, maybe my last.

I've learned all I can. I don't believe my grandfather knew there was an embezzlement going on. I don't think A.L. was capable of such deceit.

Now, I long for my own home, nestled in the sweet, soft hills of New Hampshire—hills that no longer seem claustrophobic but comforting and safe. I'm ready to put a wrap on this story. But first, before I leave, I crush the black earth in my fist, scatter it aloft, and paraphrase what my father used to say to me: "You were a bastard, George Hormel, for laying my grandfather so low."

23.

Old Papers

Hanover, New Hampshire

2001

Back in New Hampshire, the gold and red of the autumn that I returned to have released their hold and we're in "stick season," when the leaves have gone and we can see deep into our muscular forests. The temperature has dropped. The burnished light is dwindling, barely enough to hold us through winter. Snow piles gather against our driveway.

For a few months, I stow away my last visit to Austin as I finish a busy consulting season and the holidays, with kids and their friends in and out of our house.

But January comes and as we settle into winter, my desire to know more rises again.

I thought I'd wrestled this curiosity to the ground in Oak Dale Township, Iowa. Maybe, like Jay Hormel, it's just my gut telling me there's something remaining to see. A blank space that as of yet has no form. I wanted to be done. I wanted to be sure. But I'm not done, and I'm not sure.

Over coffee with Michael one morning in late January, I remember the fourth box of my grandfather's papers—a box I've never perused.

"I need to go back to Dartmouth," I say. "And go through that box."

ON THE LONG, HEAVY OAK TABLE IN THE SPECTACULAR reading room inside Rauner Special Collections Library on the Dartmouth campus, Sarah Hartwell, my companion and aide here, has placed a box for me.

Soaring multipaned windows reach above. North light pours into this room, whose stacks are moisture- and climate-controlled, and sealed to protect the old papers they house. Which makes me think back to George Hormel's dry sausage room. Here, I have a twelve-foot surface on which to spread the papers, and while the room will accommodate several dozen readers, I'm the only one here today.

"I'll leave you to it," Sarah says. She's always there for my discoveries. "Tell me what you find."

I pull out papers, flip through old bank receipts, find the deed for Burr Oaks, and thumb across cattle listings and advertisements for animals purchased and sold by the Minnesota Holstein Company. Additional correspondence with George Swift. More on the aftermath of A.L. being fired. Nothing unusual or surprising.

I keep flipping.

Then I grip an old paper and my stomach somersaults. "Shit," I say under my breath, knowing I'm not allowed to speak above a whisper and certainly shouldn't curse.

But *no.*

It's dated August 4, 1920. I quickly calculate—this is eleven months *before* Cy's embezzlement was discovered by Jay, and the year I now know Cy took $600,000—half his full steal—from the company. More than brazen, he must have been nearly manic, maybe thinking he'd surely be caught one of those days, so why not just take it all?

I hold my breath and reread the page. Then read it again. Three lines on a simple sheet of typewriter paper, the kind an old-time banker might dash off for the record. Typed by the assistant to the president at Austin's Farmers & Merchants Bank—the same president I now know didn't want to meet up with Jay Hormel; the banker who, like my grandfather, raised Holsteins on the side; the banker who presided over the account Thomson made deposits to, of Oak Dale Farms.

I have today [credited your] note of $2,817.26, together with interest of $32.90, making a total of $2,850.16. Funds to take care of this we received from Ransome J. Thomson.

What? Cy paid off my grandfather's loan? I pull out my BlackBerry for its calculator. What was $2,850.16 in 1920 would be $44,843.48 today. I let this sink in, my mind already resorting to bargaining. Did A.L. *ask* him to do it? Did Cy know A.L. had the loan and offered to pay it? Was he buying my grandfather's friendship? Or . . . trying to buy his silence?

I sit back in my chair and look away, then back at the letter. I don't know. It's certainly possible an embezzler might trade his hallmark generosity for a prior supervisor's acquiescence, even if A.L. wasn't aware of that exchange. Even if he never knew an embezzlement was going on. If A.L. were here right now, what would I ask him, and what would he say?

Prior to the discovery of Cy's embezzlement, A.L. could easily have paid off all his debts. Why would he need anyone's help? In particular, how could he justify a subordinate paying off this loan? Was that a less clear boundary back then than it is now? And, did Thomson pay off the loans of others at the company? If others benefited, should my grandfather have been any different?

I wish El were here right now. She'd have opinions for me to lean against. I will call her, but I need to go through the rest of the box.

The reading room grows dim. My chest heaves. I'm poking at long-lived family mythology here—our need to believe in powerful men. My mouth is metal. My palms are sponge. I reread the letter. A.L. and Thomson *were* linked in the way I'd hoped they were not.

Was this what V., the Hormel archivist, was alluding to? This one letter, in a box my father didn't need to preserve, changes the picture of his curated story about A.L. But did Dad even read this letter? If he did, he was silent on it. Maybe he never looked in any of these boxes because the trauma he'd experienced in Austin was too much for him to relive. Still, he considered the papers important enough to preserve for eternity in these archives.

I sit back in my chair, disillusioned by my grandfather.

But the box tempts me further. I don't want to look, but I must.

And here's another. Dated June 3, 1921, just three weeks before Cy's embezzling was discovered, a carbon copy of a letter from First National Bank in LeRoy, on whose board Merrill Chesebrough would later sit for twenty-five years, addressed to Ransome J. Thomson:

> *Your letter with checks to cover Mr. Eberhart's note and interest received this morning.*

If the first letter disillusioned me, this one levels me. My brain spins.

I rush through the rest of the box and find nothing more.

Even now, I cannot fathom that my grandfather knew Cy was embezzling, despite having always been a keen observer of those around him. Neither George Hormel nor

Cy accused him of it and these three men were cut from very different cloths. And yet, just as my father believed a woman as smart as Lena must have known about her cancer, wasn't A.L., too, smart enough to have known?

I upbraid myself for that thought, calling up the well-worn cliché about hindsight. If I'd been A.L. in 1919 and 1920, with no visible corporate or familial ghosts on the horizon, would I have been savvier? During a time when men were powerfully preoccupied with building and moving our country forward and pressured to grow companies at all cost? After the federal government's auditors through the war years and Ernst & Ernst had found nothing? George Hormel had hired and promoted a young man who reminded him of himself at a younger age—and, blind to his indiscretions, kept elevating him. Jay Hormel didn't see anything either, except by chance.

We understand the power of denial, but only after. We don't see things we don't want to see until we're in too deep. We excuse behavior we don't want to confront. We blind ourselves to realities we aren't ready to face. From 1910-1921, in Austin, Minnesota, Cy had perfectly groomed his victims, creating his own mythology that everyone wanted to believe. Comptrollers and fathers; CEOs and priests; the heads of all our most revered systems have created all kinds of myths we cling to, in denial.

Only much later would I learn about early criminologist Donald Cressey's Fraud Triangle from Eugene Soltes at Harvard Business School. Cressey argued that for embezzlement to occur, three elements needed to be present: First is an opportunity. Cy Thomson had nearly sole responsibility for, and access to, the company's cash. Second is a motivating pressure. Thomson desperately wanted to become a man in a suit, to make a place for himself in the elite class of my grandfather and George Hormel. Third, a rationalization. Maybe Thomson felt he deserved the money given all his hard work and the accolades he'd received from his superiors. Maybe he thought the company had cash to burn. Maybe employees were getting away with skimming pork chops from the packing plant.

According to Cressey, each element is heavily influenced by a company's culture. Fast growth at the Hormel company. The aftermath of a world war. Laissez-faire supervision. Too much denial and undeserved trust all around. Maybe George was right. Maybe the company had gone soft.

Light drains from the reading room. Still, my portraits of these men remain incomplete.

Maybe my grandfather was just George Hormel's fall guy. But George didn't have to seek A.L.'s removal and he didn't need to force A.L.'s resignation—that was the greedy, my-success-at-your-cost, kick-you-when-you're-down side of George—cleaving both my grandfather's livelihood and his wealth for his own benefit.

WHAT HAPPENED TO MY GRANDFATHER SHAPED both my father's and my outlook on the world, our chosen lines of work, and our approach to finances. My father retained A.L.'s fundamental trust in people through his life, a naivete that I felt sometimes harmed him. After leaving Austin for college, unlike his father, he struggled financially for many years, not obtaining a secure job until he was fifty-two years old, five years after my birth. He vigorously distrusted big companies, and especially family-owned ones. He never invested in stocks. Still, he took his inborn talent to the very top of his own field, the literary one—like father, like son.

Meanwhile, I chose a career in the business world in part, if only in retrospect, to understand my family legacy and the grandfather I never knew. Like my father, however, I've lived a financially conservative life—taking on little debt, not speculating in real estate, assuming no windfalls. A.L.'s fall from grace and my father's reaction to it likely informed those tendencies.

The day departs from this room and the early evening of a New England winter approaches, but still I sit, contemplating. What do we do with our complicated family legacies? How do we move on, in light of how much we can never know? I've found few final answers. And no easy truth.

Still, I know these things: I love my grandfather. I feel no shame in what happened. I'm proud of the parts of him that have taken root in me. He was fully human, taking his wins and losses with pragmatic resolve. He chose a self-confident, spunky woman for his bride—a grandmother I wish I could have known. His children each considered him both a strong and gentle father. His friends remained true to his end. He helped build an American company that survives to this day.

24.

Aftermath

After Lena's death, Elizabeth went to live with Adah and Ralph Crane. Two years later, my grandfather married a woman named Clara, and Elizabeth returned to live with them. My father matriculated at the University of Minnesota, then transferred to Dartmouth College and, later, for education at Cambridge University in England, and at Harvard. His older brother, Dryden, who had by then become an investment advisor and Regional Vice President of Eaton & Howard, Inc. (now Eaton Vance), assisted A.L. in winding down the sale of Burr Oaks and Whispering Pines, along with his Minnesota Holstein Company livestock. It took years—not surprising, given that the country was moving toward the Great Depression.

After heading up Dold's new meatpacking plant in Omaha, A.L. joined Albert Cross in Chicago to start the firm Cross, Roy, Eberhart, and Harris, which became the largest provision dealer in its time on the Chicago Board of Trade. Four years later, he and Clara moved to Kansas for A.L. to take a job as general manager for Dold in Wichita, a city he came to love. There, he was a member of the Community

Chest, the Rotary, the Salvation Army, Crestview Country Club, and the United Congregational Church.

In 1929, A.L. headed up sales for Gobel in New York's Meatpacking District. At the age of sixty-five, he was approached by a headhunter for a turnaround job at Hugo Arnold's flagship meatpacking plant in Chicago. He took the position, while continuing to sell car trailers on the side—a secondary interest that helped him get out into the wild places he loved most.

On July 5, 1937, at the age of sixty-nine, A.L. died in a crash when his car hit an elevated pier in downtown Chicago on a business trip. An autopsy found that he had not been drinking or speeding. His death was ruled an accident. Articles after his death credited him with many accomplishments, among them the development of many leading men in the packing industry of that time.

A.L. and Lena are buried next to each other in Oakwood Cemetery in Austin.

WITHIN TWO YEARS OF THE EMBEZZLEMENT, the value of Hormel stock reached its pre-embezzlement level and the company paid off its loans. Had A.L. been allowed to hold on to his Hormel stock through his lifetime and passed it to his heirs, it would be worth about $200 million today.

In 1929, seven years after my grandfather left Austin, George Hormel ceded control of the presidency to Jay, though he remained on the company board. Word has it he was as demanding a director as he had been a boss, expecting detailed daily reports on every aspect of the company.

In retirement, George and Lillian built themselves a mansion in Bel Air, California, and moved there. They bequeathed their Austin home to the YWCA.

Lillian Hormel died on March 23, 1946, at the age of seventy-eight. George Hormel followed three months later, on June 5, 1946, at the age of eighty-five. By the time of his death, the company he'd founded employed 6,000 people. Like my grandparents, both Hormels are buried at Oakwood Cemetery in Austin.

JAY HORMEL TOOK OVER AS PRESIDENT OF THE company in 1929. He held the reins until 1946, during which time he oversaw continued growth, along with the invention of Spam. His three sons—George "Geordie" Hormel, Thomas Dubois Hormel, and James Catherwood Hormel—each made their mark in varied careers and used their inherited wealth to contribute substantially to progressive causes including the environment, the arts, and HIV/AIDS services.

After Jay retired, the company was no longer headed by members of the Hormel family.

Jay died on August 30, 1954, in Austin. Tim Corey, who had helped Jay uncover Cy Thomson's embezzlement and recouped what little he could from Cy's assets, was named chairman of the board several months after Jay's death.

CY THOMSON WAS RELEASED FROM STILLWATER prison, in Minnesota, on March 22, 1930, and placed on parole for two years. His wife, Maude, had died in 1928, while he was incarcerated. In 1931, Cy married Mabelle Hanson. On April 17, 1934, he pleaded guilty to a misdemeanor charge of issuing a false check to the Austin Auto Company, was fined twenty-five dollars, and was ordered to serve thirty days in jail.

On August 24, 1941, at the age of fifty five, Cy Thomson and five other men from Waseca County, Minnesota, were convicted of sodomy. Cy was incarcerated for a second time in Stillwater. Sentenced to ten years, he served three. He'd dreamed of raising perfect animal bloodlines all his life, but between and after his two incarcerations, he worked in Waseca County and in Montana as the kind of farm laborer he'd assumed as a kid he would become.

Ransome J. Thomson died on January 16, 1955, at the age of sixty-eight.

25.

And the Strong Right of Human Love Was There

Austin

1921

I wish my grandfather were here so I could ask him what really happened. I try to imagine our conversation, but no clear words come to me. Maybe that doesn't matter. Maybe it's my father's words that describe best the emotions I will retain.

In the autumn of 1921, three months before A.L. was forced to resign, he drove his family into the countryside to enjoy the afternoon. They stopped at Whispering Pines, where Dryden, Dick, and Elizabeth fed their father's horses and admired his Holsteins.

Back at Burr Oaks, partway up the drive, as the sun slanted low through the apple orchard, A.L. turned off his car. His three children wandered the crisscrossing pathways of apple trees, lost in their rhythm, perhaps finding a cadence for the deep grief they already felt about their mother's worsening illness. They plucked apples from a branch and delighted in the meaty fruit. Maybe my grandfather and Lena found a moment for their personal sadness.

A.L. had things to say to his family, as by then he knew Lena had cancer and he'd just made the difficult decision to hold my father back from college to care for her. He called his children together for a family meeting among the trees.

I hope that day was a sunny one, as that's how I prefer imagining it, with light diminishing along the river that split their beloved home from the Hormel factory on the other side.

Whatever A.L. said to his children during that family meeting would be a point of no return. His responsibilities for helping right the House of Hormel would be high. Like fat drained off bacon, the embezzlement had rendered his family's finances lean and unstable. Lena's severe illness required each child, also, to do their part. As he tried to make sense of the swirling vortex around him, he did what he could to bind his family together for the onslaught he saw ahead.

Years later, my father captured that afternoon in his poem "Orchard," and it's through his words that I feel the impact of my family legacy—the tragedy of a mother's early death to cancer, the evil of an embezzler, and the mighty decisions of a company president that would ripple through generations to follow. A family privileged by love; a family exiled from all it had hoped for.

It is true, I have found, that our histories can inform us, even set us free.

If only we are ready to let them.

Orchard

I.

Lovely were the fruit trees in the evening.
We sat in the automobile all five of us
Full of the silence of deep grieving,
For tragedy stalked among the fruit trees.

Strongest was the father, of solid years,
Who set his jaw against the coming winter?
Pure, hard, strong, and infinitely gentle
For the worst that evil brings can only kill us.

Most glorious was the mother, beautiful
Who in the middle course of life was stalked?
By the stark shape of malignant disease,
And her face was holy white like all desire.

And we three, in our benumbing youngness,
Half afraid to guess at the danger there,
Looked in stillness at the glowing fruit trees,
While tumultuous passions raged in the air.

II

And the first, the father, with indomitable will
Strove in iron decision, in all human strength
With a powerful complete contempt of defeat,
Six feet of manhood and not a mark of fear.

And the next, the mother, wonderfully mild,
Wise with the wisdom that never changes,
Poured forth her love divinely magnified
We knew not by what imminent despair.

While the older brother and the younger,
Separate, yet placed in the first light
Of brutal recognition, held a trembling sister
Who knew not the trial of fortitude to come.

And in the evening, among the warm fruit trees
All of life and all of death were there,
Of pain unto death, of struggle to endure,
And the strong right of human love was there.

Postscript

After the Austin poetry celebration in October 2000, my brother and I worked with Mike Ruzek and the Austin school system to establish a permanent endowment fund with the Austin Public Education Foundation for an annual poetry contest. To this day, each year, hundreds of kindergartners through high schoolers craft and submit their poems to a panel of judges. A winning poet from each grade in each of Austin's eight schools is selected to receive a small cash prize. This contest keeps the kids of Austin experimenting with the poetic form, and learning how to submit their work for recognition.

Every April, I receive a sheaf of the winning poems. The authors each have a story to tell, and I savor their verses. Along with the school system that encourages their voices and the heart-stopping prairie land of southern Minnesota, I will be forever tethered to Austin.

*Receive bonus content when you sign up
for Gretchen's newsletter at www.gretchencherington.com.*

Acknowledgments

Books that served as primary source materials and to which I am greatly indebted include: *In Quest of Quality: Hormel's First 75 Years* and *The Hormel Legacy: 100 Years of Quality*, both by Richard Dougherty, commissioned and published by Geo. A. Hormel & Company; *The Open Road*, by George A. Hormel, unpublished version; *Cy Thomson— The Generous Embezzler*, compiled by Eileen Evans; *The Yankee of the Yards*, by Louis F. Swift and Arthur Van Vlissengen, Jr.; *Too Big to Fail: The Inside Story of How Wall Street and Washington Fought to Save the Financial System—and Themselves*, by Andrew Ross Sorkin; *The Chain: Farm, Factory, and the Fate of Our Food*, by Ted Genoways; and *Why They Do It: Inside the Mind of the White-Collar Criminal*, by Eugene Soltes. In addition, I have consulted hundreds of internet sources, too numerous to list.

Eloise Eberhart Chevrier, if you hadn't invited me to Austin in 1995, this book would not exist. With your sister, Elizabeth Eberhart Moffat, you've inspired me through a lifetime and honored my search for truth through two memoirs. I love you both.

In Austin, I was generously befriended by Knowles Dougherty, Ella Marie Lausen, and Merrill Chesebrough, each now deceased. Perhaps without knowing it, these three helped me form a backbone for this story. I'm saddened the book was not completed in time for them to read it. Also vital in Austin have been Mike Ruzek, Kari Bain, Jeni Lindberg, and Sue Doocy. With special thanks to the Mower County Historical Society for its records and archivists.

Among my first readers were my critique partners, Shelley Blanton-Stroud, Ashley Sweeney, and Debra Thomas. You each inspire me to write better and you answered every call when I was stuck. To think that we've collectively produced four new books during the eighteen months of COVID! Our mutual commitment to writing and friendship brings out the best in each of us.

Soul sister Ellen Schecter, you have read nearly every draft of both my books and through more than a decade. I wouldn't want to be a writer, or live my life, without you.

I was lucky to have equally high-quality beta readers and proofers. Bob Bowers, Elizabeth Garber, Nora Kells Gordon, Sarah Martel, Deborah K. Shepherd, and Andrew Stroud, thank you for helping me turn this book toward what it is now.

To my readers of *Poetic License*, friends and fans—how lucky you have made me. It's for you that I explore complex family stories and support all women in claiming their innate power to tell theirs.

Brooke Warner, you and your phenomenal team at She Writes Press have given me the perfect publishing home. Especially you, forever and always, for taking a first risk on me, and for being a woman I wildly admire. And to my terrific team at SWP: Shannon Green, editorial manager; Julie Metz, cover designer; Krissa Lagos, copyeditor; Katie Caruana, proofreader; and Tabitha Lahr, book designer. Big thanks to Crystal Patriarche, Tabitha Bailey, and the publicity team at BookSparks. Thanks, also, for marketing strategy and support from Sue Campbell at Pages and Platforms.

To my children, Ben Cherington and Molly Cherington—your lives and minds, your laughter and love, inspire me daily, and I'm prouder than tongue can tell to be your mom. Your support for this third career is especially appreciated.

And to Michael, my first and last reader; ever insightful; and the best listener as I read aloud and you suggest the right improvements. You help make every day a story of truth and love.

About the Author

Gretchen Cherington grew up in a home filled with literary icons from Robert Frost to Anne Sexton to James Dickey. Her first memoir, *Poetic License*, won first runner-up in memoir for the 2021 Eric Hoffer Award and was a 2021 Foreword INDIES finalist in Autobiography and Memoir. Like her grandfather, she chose a long career in business, advising hundreds of CEOs in how to transform their companies into places where both business and people could thrive. She was adjunct faculty in business school executive programs at Harvard, Dartmouth, and Columbia. Gretchen has served on twenty boards, and has chaired four, including a multibillion-dollar B-corporation bank, winning her two leadership awards. Her undergraduate and MBA degrees were earned from the University of New Hampshire. Cherington's essays have appeared in *Huffington Post*, *Yankee*, *Electric Lit*, *Hippocampus*, and *Quartz*, and she has been nominated for a Pushcart Prize. Gretchen and her husband split their time between Portland, Maine, and a saltwater cottage on Penobscot Bay where fading paint is the norm and her gardens have to manage themselves. When not working on her next book, she can be found in her hiking boots, on her bikes or skis out in the wild. For more, please see www.gretchencherington.com.

Author photo © Chris Milliman

Also by Gretchen Cherington

POETIC LICENSE

At age forty, Gretchen Cherington, daughter of Pulitzer Prize–winning poet Richard Eberhart, faced a dilemma: Should she protect her parents' well-crafted family myths while continuing to silence her own voice? Or was it time to challenge those myths and speak her truth? In *Poetic License*, Cherington bravely and candidly retraces her past to make sense of her father and herself.

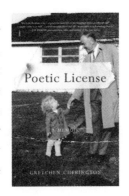

"Richard Eberhart was a generous man but, as his daughter shows, a difficult and complex person as well. This is a vivid memoir, flaws and all, and Gretchen Cherington has crafted a narrative worth reading closely."

—JAY PARINI, poet, novelist, critic, and author
of *The Last Station: A Novel of Tolstoy's Last Year*

Print ISBN: 978-1-63152-711-1 | $16.95
E-ISBN: 978-1-63152-712-8 | $9.95
www.shewritespress.com

SELECTED TITLES FROM SHE WRITES PRESS

She Writes Press is an independent publishing company founded to serve women writers everywhere. Visit us at www.shewritespress.com.

Someday Mija, You'll Learn the Difference Between a Whore and a Working Woman: A Memoir by Yvonne Martinez. $17.95, 978-1-64742-102-1. Intergenerational trauma is transformed into resilience and post traumatic growth in this gripping story of brutal domestic violence, family secrets, and uncommon wisdom. After Yvonne Martinez is taken in by her dying, once-prostitute grandmother, she later learns that her grandmother was long ago trafficked by her own mother in depression-era Utah—a revelation that sends Yvonne on a search for answers ends in healing . . . and in her becoming an activist.

On the Ledge: A Memoir by Amy Turner. $17.95, 978-1-64742-225-7. After Amy Turner is mowed down by a pickup truck, she struggles to heal the trauma of her own brush with death—a process that, unexpectedly and despite her resistance, forces her to confront a childhood trauma she thought she resolved long ago: the morning her father climbed onto a fifty-foot-high ledge outside his hotel window and threatened to jump, an event that made national news.

Implosion: Memoir of an Architect's Daughter by Elizabeth W. Garber. $16.95, 978-1-63152-351-9. When Elizabeth Garber, her architect father, and the rest of their family move into Woodie's modern masterpiece, a glass house, in 1966, they have no idea that over the next few years their family's life will be shattered—both by Woodie's madness and the turbulent 1970s.

Many Hands Make Light Work: A Memoir by Cheryl Stritzel McCarthy. $16.95, 978-1-63152-628-2. A rollicking family of nine children, offspring of an eccentric professor father and unflappable mother, paint, spackle, and eventually rebuild a dozen tumbledown old houses in their Midwest college town in the 1960s and '70s—and, at odd moments, break into song, because they sing as they work, like a von Trapp family in painters caps.